FROM
DEATH TO LIFE

Other works by the Author:

Lord, When? A Biblical Perspective of The Second Coming

FROM
DEATH TO LIFE

JOHN J. COBB

iUniverse, Inc.
Bloomington

From Death to Life

iUniverse books may be ordered through booksellers or by contacting:

iUniverse
1663 Liberty Drive
Bloomington, IN 47403
www.iuniverse.com
1-800-Authors (1-800-288-4677)

ISBN: 978-1-4759-0533-5 (sc)
ISBN: 978-1-4759-0535-9 (hc)
ISBN: 978-1-4759-0534-2 (ebk)

Printed in the United States of America

iUniverse rev. date: 07/10/2012

CONTENTS

LIST OF ILLUSTRATIONS AND DIAGRAMS

PREFACE

One of the most shattering experience in any person life is the realization that everything they had been taught was a lie! This was my experience when I accepted Jesus Christ as my savior at the age of twelve. Like Luther's quest for the true meaning of justification, I longed to know more about the Lord Jesus Christ and the tremendous change that had come over me. Unfortunately, my desire remained unfilled because Christian education in my church, whether in Sunday school or weekly bible studies, lacked content and quality in the area of biblical doctrine.

To be fair, this was not entirely our teachers' fault, since they were a product of their time and circumstances that came with unique challenges of their own. Though I was saved in a small church in a small town in Alabama, I moved to the south side of Chicago in the early 60's, where I spent my teenage years. Like many churches in the inner city, ours did not have the luxury of having the best teaching aids, curriculum, or teachers for our Sunday school. As a result, we were not exposed to the foundational doctrines of the Christian faith in their purest form. Therefore, biblical literacy in this area was lacking, or not as strong as it needed to be in many churches during that period.

Unfortunately, this left young people like myself prime candidates for the popular cult of that time; the Jehovah Witnesses. Without a proper understanding of the basic doctrines of Christianity, such as; who is God, who is Christ and what does it mean to be saved, I was easily drawn into this cult when the opportunity presented itself.

At that time, I welcomed my relationship with the Jehovah Witnesses, because I viewed their teachings as a medium of learning more about God and his word. For three years, I sat under their teachings, attended their halls, and received instructions from their Bible and periodicals about God, his kingdom and the life he has for us; yet my soul felt unfulfilled and strangely empty. It wasn't until the end of my third year with them that God revealed to me, they were not Christians at all; but wolves in sheep clothing. I could not believe how easily they had deceived, and indoctrinated me in a gospel contrary to the New Testament; mainly, denying the deity of Jesus Christ and his redemptive work (Galatians 1:6)!

The reason many cults, such as the Jehovah Witnesses, are able to deceive and indoctrinate young Christians (and adults) so easily, is because they are not grounded doctrinally. In other words, there was nothing unusual about my thirst for biblical knowledge as an adolescent! The bible makes it clear that once we're born again, our natural tendency is to yearn for God's Word (I Peter 2:2). Unfortunately, the Devil is well aware of this fact and therefore, thrilled when newly converted men and women, boys and girls are deprived of the deeper truths and principles found only in God's Word!

Though this book is one among millions on the great doctrines of the Christian faith, I believe it to be unique in two ways. First, it is written to the Christian who find themselves in the same situation as I was when the Lord saved me; seeking to know and understand the magnificence, glory, and wondrous love of our God. In a sense, it is written to laymen from a layman's perspective.

Second, as I see it, the Church has become more concerned about solving social and economic problems than teaching the fundamental doctrines of our faith. As a result, many Christians are poorly equipped to defend their faith against the teachings of cults and false teachers.

While there does exist a need to tackle social and economic injustice, these were never meant to be the church's central focus. Her focus and message, regardless of race or denomination, must always be Christ centered! When this focus is vague, lost, or compromised, the effectiveness of the Church to be salt and light to a lost and dying world is severely hampered, or at best ineffective!

The doctrines and principles given in God's Word are essential to the spiritual well-being of each Christian and finally the Universal Church. When writing to Titus, Paul tells him to teach 'sound doctrine' (Titus 1:9). The Greek word translated as 'sound' in Titus 1:9 means healthy. Paul's argument to Titus (and us through him) is this: since Jesus Christ chose Christians to manifest himself to the world; Christians must develop themselves through 'sound doctrine'!

In essence, God has given the world three things. First, He gave his only begotten Son Jesus Christ to save the world from their sin (Matthew 1:21; John 3:16). Second, he gave to the world the Universal Church to live in unity in and among them in order that the world might see his love for them. Finally, he gave the words of life to Christians in the form of the Holy Bible, so they could tell sinners the good news of his saving grace and mercy. All three are made possible only by and through the life, death and resurrection of Jesus Christ!

Included throughout this book are; diagrams, graphics and illustrations to help bring out the truths of what I believe to be key doctrines every Christian should be familiar with. Additionally, books of the Bible are spelled out in order to avoid confusing books with similar names and to assist those who may not be familiar with abbreviated names.

The reader will note that phrases, statements and truths are stated in one chapter and repeated in another. This is intentional and designed to connect, explain, or help the reader better understand how one doctrine relates to another. For example, truths discussed in the chapter on sin are also discussed in the chapter involving Adam and Eve's sin in the garden. This is done to help clarify the role sin played in their disobedience of God's command. To further highlight the meanings of doctrines contained in this writing, key words have been italicized.

This book is the result of positive feedback received from attendees of workshops and classes I've conducted on foundational doctrines of the Christian faith. Their interest and enthusiasm was the prime motivator for putting much of what I have taught in written form. The Bible teaches that every Christian is gifted by God (I Corinthians 12). Though not stated explicitly, I believe that along with the gift comes the passion and energy needed to hone and perfect it, in order that it might edify the body of Christ.

God has not only gifted me, and given me a passion, in the area of biblical doctrine, he has also afforded me the opportunity to serve his people as keynote speaker at conventions, as well as, writing and teaching expositional classes at our church. Additionally, I am privileged to serve as one of the writers for Adult Curriculum for the *Baptist Laymen*, published by the National Baptist Convention USA, Inc. Finally, I had the opportunity to complete courses from the Ligonier School of Theology in Ontario Canada (no longer active), on *The Holy Spirit*, *The Cross of Christ*, and *The Holiness of God*.

As I look back on my experience with the Jehovah Witnesses, I see how in his providence, God allowed me to experience the dangers of being fascinated by the Jehovah Witnesses without being ensnared by their false gospel. When I think of this experience and God's deliverance, I must echo David's words recorded in Psalms 116, "What shall I render unto the LORD for all his benefits toward me" (v. 12)? *From Death to Life,* is a part of my rendering to God, for all the benefits he continues to provide for me. In some small way, I join with others in sounding the battle trumpet to awaken Christians to the dangers of neglecting the teaching of sound doctrine (Titus 1:9)!

My hope and prayer is that, *From Death to Life* will not only be read by Christian, but those whose soul the Spirit of God has already begun to awaken from sin and death. As they read of the wonder of God's holiness, the author's desire and prayer is that they too will be quickened by the Holy Spirit, who will awaken them to the realization of the enormous debt owed to God!

There are words used in *From Death to Life,* which may offend or sound harsh to some. The author's use of such words is not to offend, but lovingly expose to both sinner and saint alike of the dark and hopeless realm in which we all lived prior to God's manifestation of grace in our lives. This is the basis for such words: to see ourselves, not as individuals deserving God's love, grace, and mercy, but as people rightly deserving his wrath, judgment and an eternity in the lake of fire.

Finally, I want to thank the following people for their time and energy in providing recommendations for the book; verifying biblical passages for clarity, accuracy, and appropriateness, and the many hours devoted to. Their contributions in this endeavor were critical in maintaining the integrity and truths within this book.

My Wife, Fay Cobb
My Pastor, Walstone Francis
Loretta Henton
Darryl Strong
Shawn Holmes
Todd McClern

PRINCIPAL ABBREVIATIONS

ASV American Standard Version
GW God's Word Translation of the Bible
JFB Jamieson, Fausett, and Brown Commentary
NICOT New International Commentary on the Old Testament
NIV New International Version

INTRODUCTION

The conscience is a unique entity. Though informed by the intellect, it is not part of the mind. Though it aids us in making ethical decisions, it is not part of the will. However, both are crucial in shaping and informing it. Regarding the importance of the conscience, Dr. John MacArthur writes that the conscience, ". . . is the automatic warning system that tells us, 'Pull up! Pull up'! before we crash and burn. (MacArthur, John F. Jr. *The Vanishing Conscience, Drawing the Line In A No-Fault, Guilt Free World.* Dallas, London, Vancouver, Melbourne: Word Publishing, 1994, 36)

This might explains why someone has said, "The Church is the conscience of society"; because like the human conscience, the Church acts as society's warning system, sounding the alarm when it strays away from what is moral, right and just! After all, only the Church is privy to God's special revelation that reveals his will for humanity, plan of salvation and principles needed to maintain proper decency and order in any society.

Unfortunately, because the church in many parts of the world seems reluctant to take a firm position on key biblical teachings, such as; the holiness of God, the deity of Christ and his redemptive work, marriage as defined by God, and other ethical issues that define her, she finds herself in an extremely precarious position. In other words, the Church is more than a building; it is a spiritual organism consisting of Christians united by the Holy Spirit into the one Lord, Jesus Christ (Ephesians 4:4-6)! As such, she stands alone as the sole entity that understands that all the problems faced by society are spiritual in nature; and therefore, can only be resolved through spiritual means.

Too many Christians today, ignore or fail to emphasize absolutes found in the Bible. This, combined with the desire to become inoffensive to non-Christians has led to the Church losing its uniqueness. When the line defining the differences between the Church and the world is removed or is not clear, the Church's authority as society's moral compass is significantly decreased. This probably explains why the Church in

America has almost become irrelevant; not because it has lost its salvation, but because she has become unsure of her identity and purpose as given in the Holy Bible.

Paul highlights the importance of the Bible in these words from 2 Timothy 3:16, "All Scripture is inspired by God" (2 Timothy 3:16). Based on this and other verses in the Bible, Christians can rely on the assurance that whatever the Bible declares is trustworthy, because it has God as its source!

While man played a vital role in its development, that role was purely coincidental and of God's choice. In other words, though men wrote the books of the Bible using their own unique talents, knowledge, and experiences, the sum of its contents originated from the breath of God! Regarding the origin of the Bible in 2 Timothy 3:16, John Calvin writes, "This is a principle which distinguishes our religion from all others". Calvin continues his comments about the same verse, ". . . we know that God has spoken to us, and are fully convinced that the prophets did not speak at their own suggestion, but that, being organs of the Holy Spirit, they only uttered what they had been commissioned from heaven to proclaim. Whoever then wishes to profit in the Scriptures, let him, first of all, lay down this as a settled point, that the Law and the Prophets are not a doctrine delivered according to the will and pleasure of men, but dictated by the Holy Spirit". (Institutes IV, viii, 9)

Many conclude from Calvin's statement that he believed in a dictation theory of inspiration; which stress that the writers of the bible were nothing more than stenographers. However, nothing could be further from the truth! In making this statement, Calvin and others like him were not lending their voices of support to the dictation theory of Inspiration. Instead, their teaching and preaching stemmed from a deep reverence of God, his supremacy, his sovereignty, and his holiness.

The point behind the statements in the last paragraph was done, not to elevate Calvin, but to shed further information and clarity on the subject regarding the origin of God's Word. In other words, though Calvin's passion and extensive knowledge of God's Word are indisputable, I agree with others (and even Calvin himself), that the church stands on God's Word alone!

Apart from God's Word, there is nothing, to tell us about sin; its impact on humanity, and God's sending his only begotten Son to redeem us. Without God's Word, there is no faith, and where faith is missing, there is no possibility of salvation! That is the importance and power of God's Word to the Christian. It is bread to our soul, a lamp to our feet and the mirror by which God reveals himself to us. These realities of holy Scripture empowered a lone monk named Martin Luther to stand boldly against an entire empire, and the false church behind it, and declared, "Unless I am persuaded by Scripture alone, I will not recant"!

Such passion and love for God's Word is sorely missing in Christendom today. This is one of the reasons (if not the main reason); the Church has lost her impact on society. But how did the church arrive at this point? First (and these are solely the author's opinion), the Church has lost sight of God's holiness! This is the reason many of our churches look more like halls or theaters than the place where the people of God come together to meet the holy One. Pulpits, pews; stained glass windows and crosses have long been replaced by theater seating, stages, lecterns and buildings less 'offensive' to the world.

While many regard these as only symbolic of the past, they are the unique objects and fixtures that set the church building apart from all others. When one enters a church, they should know they are entering a holy place, and a place of reverence. It is not just because it's Sunday, nor even because the people of God are there (although both are true), but because it's set apart for worship of a holy God! Like a lighthouse, it's the one building in any community that distinguishes itself as the sole truth declaring, "This is the way"!

As a child, I knew Sunday was a special day and different from any other because there were special shoes and clothes worn only on Sunday. When we met for worship back then, a spirit of love and joy characterized the assembly; and even though I'm older now, I remember those days and in a way, long for them!

Because a sense of God's holiness has been lost, it inevitably leads to this Second cause, compromising of our faith. In an effort to save the world, we have compromised the integrity of the pure message Jesus Christ commissioned us to proclaim. In other words, evangelism no longer begins with a focus on humanity's fallen condition before a holy, righteous and just God; but instead on the assumption that all people are somehow seeking and desiring to know God. As a result, evangelism begins and ends, not with God's mercy and grace, but his love; sin and its impact on humanity and God intolerance of it, is rarely mentioned!

This is not the message of Jesus (Matthew 4:17), or Pentecost (Acts 2:1-38), or Paul (Romans 3:10-12)! The truth in all these passages is humanity's natural hatred of God and His Law. This is every human being's condition when born into the world, and the Gospel is the only source that reveals it!

Not only does it reveal our sin, it provides the only remedy—Jesus Christ! Only after people are brought face-to-face to their vileness, corruptness, sinfulness and worthiness of Hell, will they call out, "Men and brethren, what shall we do" (Acts 2:37)?

Third, the church has lost its impact on society because doctrine is de-emphasized. How does a group of people identify themselves? Is it not through its teachings? How does a group of people live out their lives? Is it not by adhering to principles and truths that are defined in their teachings?

When instructing Timothy about the importance of Scripture in nurturing those he leads, Paul did not just focus on his skills. Instead, he reminded him that, "All Scripture is inspired by God". Paul highlights this aspect of Scripture to emphasize the fact that the authority, integrity, and reliability of any principle or law rest solely on the character of the person giving them. In the case of the Bible, because God is its author, we can take all the words written within it as authoritative and the only source of truths that governs the life of the Christian!

For this reason, Paul tells Timothy that Scripture is, "profitable for doctrine". God's Word reveals all that the Church needs to know about himself, creation, his Law, Jesus Christ, the Holy Spirit, redemption, humanity, creation, the future of the world and the second coming. As Paul told the Christians living in Rome during the first century, one does not need to go to the ends of the world to find truth (Romans 10:6, 7); it's right before us in God's Word (Romans 10:8).

Not only is God's Word profitable for doctrine, it is also profitable, or useful, for reproof. The church is faced with much error today, both within and without. The only means she has to expose and test false teachings is God's Word (Titus 1:9-11)!

Not only is Scripture profitable for doctrine and reproof; it is useful for correction. Do you want to live morally and ethical, pleasing both God and men? Read, meditate and understand the Scriptures, for in them are the principles that lead to a transformed heart, capable of producing a godly life.

Finally, Scripture is profitable for instructions in righteousness. There is much confusion today about what is right and wrong. This is because society refuses to accept objective truth, but has resorted to relativism; which seeks all truth from within a heart and soul corrupted and controlled by sin. As the Bible declares, who can trust, believe or expect such a thing to produce truth (Jeremiah 17:9)! This is the true source of all manner of sexual deviancy, crimes, pornography, and all sorts of evil and selfishness. The way of righteousness is only found in God's Word!

THE STRUCTURE OF THE BOOK

There are several key doctrines that define the Christian faith. Those selected in, *From Death to Life* are the ones I believe to be critical in developing a thorough understanding of God and the vast abyss from which he saves us. Because of this, I felt it only natural that the first chapter focus should be on God's holiness. This attribute not only sets him apart from all else; it separates him from everything and everyone sinful! Moses and David were two Old Testament characters whose lives illustrate this truth about God's character and his intolerance of sin (Numbers 20:8–12; 2 Samuel 11, 12).

At the end of chapter one, the reader should not only come away with some concept of God's holiness, but how awful and dreadful is this force called sin. This is the subject of chapters two through four. Chapter two looks at the definition of sin; its control over humanity, and how it operates in and through us.

Having established what sin is and the extent of its power, chapter three introduce us to Satan, or the Devil. As God's archenemy, Satan's goal remains that of deceiving mankind (and angels), through deception, lies and subtlety. In this chapter, we learn how Satan accomplished this act of deception through Adam and Eve causing them to disobey God, and God's ensuing judgment. I mentioned earlier that two Old Testament examples of God's hatred of sin were seen in the life of Moses and David. However, there can be no greater revelation of God's hatred for sin than the judgment imposed on Adam and Eve for their sin.

Since Adam's sin in the Garden of Eden, evil has become progressively worse. Despite all the solutions offered and tried by societies all over the world, a cure for this malady continues to elude man. That is the subject of chapter four; identifying the source of all evil. Like any sickness, a cure is not possible until the cause is determined. Therefore, in this chapter, we discover the fact that the source of all evil is the sin force. Additionally, this chapter looks at the sin force's operation in humans, and explains why it is the sole source of humanity's spiritual separation from God. At the end of this chapter, the reader hopefully will understand why all efforts by people, governments, and groups to stop, or bring evil under control is futile!

Faced with the dilemma of evil and humanity's inability to do anything lasting about it, what is man to do? The answer to that question is the subject of chapters five through fourteen. Chapter five begins with the reality that since man is incapable of solving the problem of sin, God himself stepped in and did it for a select group of people. Chapter five opens by unfolding this extraordinary mystery by defining this select group of people as 'the elect'. We also learn that God chose these elect people before he made the world and will sustain them until the day they die (Ephesians 1:4)!

Furthermore, Abraham and the nation of Israel are pictures of this election and how people are saved; not by their power but the underlying working of the power of God working in and through them! As the judgment of Adam and Eve was the greatest manifestation of God's hatred of sin; so God's election of evil people is the greatest proof of his love, grace, and mercy!

This leads to the obvious question, do we chose Jesus Christ to be saved, or must he choose us first? Answers to these two questions are given in chapter six through the use of targeted passages of Scripture from the New Testament. By examining Jesus Christ's own words, we discover that no person can come to Jesus apart from God drawing them to him (Jesus). Chapter six also examines common objections to this teaching.

Chapters seven and eight continues this teaching regarding God's election by looking at God's foreknowledge. I devote two chapters to this teaching because of the confusion between God's foreknowledge and his omniscience. Chapter seven deals with the issue of omniscience, while chapter eight deals more specifically with foreknowledge. The intent of both chapters is to emphasize God's sovereignty; that is, his authority and power, to do as he please with his creation!

Predestination is one teaching that is not only misunderstood, but often ignored. This precious doctrine is one of the Christian's greatest assurances that once a person is saved, they can never be lost. Chapter nine deals with predestination by first defining its necessity as well as what it is and is not. The biblical account of Joseph is used as an illustration to help the reader understand this complex doctrine.

Seen in chapters five through nine are the Godward part of salvation. Chapters ten and eleven deal with how God enables the sinner to respond to the gospel message. Chapter ten began by identifying the fact that two agents are involved in bringing a person to the point of accepting God's call to salvation. We learn in chapter ten that the Holy Spirit is the first agent.

The second agent; the word of God is the subject of chapter eleven. Both chapters not only identify these two agents, but explain how they efficaciously work in a person's life to bring about salvation.

Up to this point, the question of how God saves us and how we are able to respond to his call has been dealt with. However, what has not been answered is the question: how did God deals with the sin issue? In other words, nothing has been said from chapters five through eleven that addressed the sin issue. As a result, the reader might rightly conclude, or at least assume, that sinful people are reunited with a holy God, while still in their sin!

The answer to this seemingly dilemma is that; God pardons the sinner by charging their sin to another person, Jesus Christ. This is the subject of chapter twelve; the doctrine of justification, where we look at its meaning, as well as key terms associated with it; such as propitiation, imputation, forensic, and other key terms. This chapter also stress that justification is an act done entirely by God! At the end of this chapter, the reader will better understand why Christians are regarded as 'saint and sinner' at the same time!

Does this mean that the person God saves has no role in his or her salvation? As far as the person being freed from the power and penalty of sin, the answer is yes! However, the reader learned in chapter twelve that justification is purely spiritual and therefore, does not affect them internally. If we are to become more like Jesus Christ and God, we must now began to allow the Holy Spirit to begin the renewal process within us as we read, study and meditate on God's Word. This ongoing process is called sanctification and is the subject of chapter thirteen.

But is this all there is to salvation; being elected, predestined, called, justified, and being transformed into a better person? Thank God, all those things discussed thus far are not the end of salvation, for God has a purpose to it all: to make us perfect and ultimately transform us into the form of Jesus Christ! Chapter fourteen is a discussion about this ultimate purpose of God for all Christians. At the end of this chapter, the reader will learn in what way will the Christian be like Christ when he returns!

Finally, the book ends with an Epilog summarizing the purpose of *From Death to Life*. I began the book by talking about the church as the conscience of society. The purpose of the statement was to highlight the Church's role in society and finally in the world. The reason that her role has become so difficult is because the Church lack a deeper understanding of God's holiness, the depth of sin from which he brought us, and the manifestation of his love in saving us from our sin!

If such benefits were granted to any of us by a stranger, we would never cease to express our gratitude. How much then should we joyfully and willingly render to God our gratitude and thankfulness for all he has done to save us, by giving ourselves to him (Psalms 116:12; Romans 12:1)! The extent to which the first century Church gave themselves to being salt and light in their society had a fundamental impact upon those around them (Acts 17:3-6). Let us pray that such fervor and resolution becomes our banner so that we also can turn our world upside down!

CHAPTER 1

Holy, Holy, Holy

"Who shall not fear thee, O Lord, and glorify Thy name? For Thou only art holy" (Revelation 15:4). When talking or writing about God, and his relationship to man, his *holiness* must always be paramount in the speaker or writer's mind. Moses declares holiness as the excellency of the divine nature; our God is "glorious in holiness" (Exodus 15:11). This is behind the prophet Habakkuk's statement, "Thou art of purer eyes than to behold evil, and canst not look upon iniquity" (Habakkuk 1:13). This is not to suggest that God's *holiness* is superior to his other attributes. Such a statement would not only be in error, but destroys the truth of his unitary nature.

Instead, the intended truth is to highlight the fact that this attribute is, "The glory of all the rest: as it is the glory of the Godhead". (Pink, Arthur. *The Attributes of God*. Grand Rapids, Michigan: Baker Books, 1975, 45) Holiness is a, "transcendental attribute", that, "runs through the rest, and cast luster upon then. It is an attribute of attributes". (Pink, *Attributes*, 45) However, though God's *holiness* accentuates his other attributes, we must never separate or see it as working apart from them.

Without *holiness*, God would still be almighty, all wise, all knowing, and sovereign over all creation. But how would such a being respond to his creatures? I'm reminded of the characterization of the mystical Greek god Zeus, who always acted impulsively to accomplish his purposes. He had little or no regard for the needs of those in the world. The people were mere puppets in Zeus' hands, with no distinctions made between the righteous or wicked, right or wrong! That is the essence of a god without *holiness*!

1

HOLINESS: THE CHIEF ATTRIBUTE OF GOD?

Regarding the importance of holiness, Arthur Pink provides this quote from the seventeenth century Puritan, Stephen Charnock, "As sincerity is the luster of every grace in a Christian, so is purity the splendor of every attribute in the Godhead. His justice is a holy justice, his wisdom a 'holy wisdom', his arm of power a 'holy power' (Psalms 98:1), his truth or promises are 'holy promise' (Psalms 105:42), and most important of all, his name is, 'holy'" (1 Chronicles 16:10, 35; Psalms 99:3; 106:47). (Pink, *Attributes*, 45)

God's *holiness* and its significance are what sets him apart from his creatures, he is "holy, holy, holy" (Isaiah 6:3). Unlike the gods conjured up by men, he is goodness, purity and perfection in its purest form; so much so that, of all the names given to him in Scripture, *holiness* trumps them all. God is the 'Holy one of Israel'; the 'Holy one' (2 Kings 19:22; Job 6:10; Psalms 16:10; 22:3; 71:22; 89:18; Isaiah 1:4; 5:19) and his name is 'holy' (1 Chronicles 16:10, 35; Psalms 99:3; 106:47).

Not only does *holiness* characterize his person, it also characterizes objects, buildings and people set apart unto him; they are all regarded as *holy* things (Exodus 29:29; 30:25; Leviticus 16:4; 27:28, 32), his people are a holy nation, a holy people and a royal priesthood (Leviticus 11:44; 20:7; Deuteronomy 7:6; 14:2; I Peter 1:15,16; 2:5:9). These are but a few examples of the Bible's description of God's *holiness*. There are many more just as accurate and just as straightforward, with the specific purpose of setting before us God's holiness (Isaiah 10:17; 41:14; 43:3, 14, 16, 20; Jeremiah 51:5; Ezekiel 39:7; Daniel 4:24; Hosea 11:9; Habakkuk 1:12; 3:3).

Finally, God's holiness highlight his perfect righteousness in all his actions, it is, "the very antithesis of all moral blemish or defilement". (Pink, *Attributes*, 45) There is no suggestion or possibility of evil ever being part of his character. As the Apostle John declares, he "is light, and in him is no darkness at all" (I John 1:5). Therefore, of necessity he must hate and punish all sin, regardless of its form or intention (Proverbs 3:32; 15:26; Nahum 1:2).

The Righteous Demands of Holiness

We understand the seriousness of God's hatred for sin in Adam and Eve's banishment from their ideal home, not for committing many sins, but for a single sin! This is not the only instance where God's *holiness* and hatred of sin are highlighted. For example, because of one sin, Moses lost the opportunity to enter Canaan; Elisha's servant was smitten with leprosy and Ananias and his wife Sapphira was struck dead for lying to the Holy Spirit! (Pink, *Attributes,* 47) And who can forget poor Uzzah, who with the sincerest of intentions and motivation dared touch God's Holy Ark, an act paid for with his life (I Chronicle 13:9-10).

These illustrations of God's *holiness* and intolerance of sin are different from the picture portrayed by the unsaved and many Christians today. To them, God is tolerant, understanding of our weaknesses and just overlooks sin. However, as seen in the lives of Moses and others; he is above all holy and, "a consuming fire" (Hebrews 12:28-29). No one can approach or see him in their defiled and corrupt state because he is unlike fallen humanity, in character and temperament (Psalms 50:21)!

God's Character: The Perfect Portrait Of Holiness

Perhaps no greater passage in all of Scripture reveals this as clearly as does the sixth chapter of Isaiah. The imagery is so powerful and awe inspiring that the reader can almost picture themselves in the temple alongside the prophet when reading this passage. I believe this is done intentionally to illustrate the difference between holiness and unholiness and the appropriate response of the individual when confronting 'the Holy God'!

The chapter opens with the words, "In the year that king Uzziah died I saw also the Lord sitting upon a throne" (Isaiah 6:1). King Uzziah was one of the greatest kings of the Southern Kingdom. His leadership and innovations and weaponry of war had catapulted Judah to prominence in every possible way (2 Chronicles 26). He made the nation safe and the peoples' hearts were at peace.

Uzziah became like many who become wealthy and powerful; filled with pride. In his pride, he dared to go into the holy place and perform duties reserved only for the priest. As a result, God immediately struck him with leprosy (2 Samuel 6:1). The once-great king's failure to reverence the things set apart unto God not only condemned him, it stripped him of his throne and doomed him to die a leper's death. This is the event that forms the background of the sixth chapter of Isaiah.

After reading this passage about Isaiah's experience in the temple, the biblical critic might wrongly believe they have found a direct contradiction in Scripture, especially after the earlier emphasis on man's inability to look at God's face and live. However, remember, we are talking about God, who can sustain those whom he want to reveal himself.

In other words, throughout the Old Testament, God often allowed various individuals to look at him. Most often, we see them as "an element of encouragement and confirmation" as He did for Hagar (Genesis 16:9-13), Jacob (Genesis 28:13-25), Moses, Aaron, Nadab and Abihu, seventy of the elders of Israel (Exodus 24:9-11) and many others. The privilege of seeing God empowered and assured his messengers and spokesmen of their commission and his approval. (Oswalt, John S. *The New International Commentary on the Old Testament, The Book of Isaiah.* Grand Rapids, Michigan: Eerdmans, 1986, 177) Isaiah was one of those individuals.

Prophets were sent by God sometimes to warn his people, or to declare his judgment on them and the nation if they did not repent from their wicked ways. The words declared were never their words, but the words of the LORD! Therefore, he and all the peoples, needed to be sure God had sent them.

This was particularly important in Isaiah's case; because Judah, God's *holy* nation was chosen (Deuteronomy 7:6) and set apart as a light to the nations around them. But now she had become arrogant and idolatrous! Their hearts were at best one of indifference towards God because they had forgotten his holiness, and his command for them to be *holy*. To get their hearts and mind back on track and fulfill his purpose through them (Isaiah 43:8-14; 49:5,6), they first needed to understand his holiness.

To help them, God would not use a 'Mount Sinai experience' (Exodus 19). Instead, he would show this truth to one man, Isaiah; and through him, arouse the whole nation. For such a task, the man of God himself had to have a personal encounter with God and his holiness.

Remember, their king had just died, therefore, the kingdom must have been in mourning. Their minds were most likely preoccupied; not only because of their tremendous loss, but the pending dangers posed by powerful enemies around them who threatened their existence. What were to become of them now that their king was no longer their protector?

Such circumstances prepared the people's hearts for the change God had in mind. His first act was to reveal himself to Isaiah who described him as, "sitting on a throne, high and lifted up, and his train filled the temple" (Isaiah 6:1). Jamieson, Fausset and Brown offers this explanation of Isaiah's location in regards to the Temple, "Isaiah is outside, near the altar in front of the temple. The doors are supposed to open, and the veil hiding the Holy of Holies to be withdrawn, unfolding to his view a vision of God" (Illustration 1). (*JFB*, Isaiah 6:1)

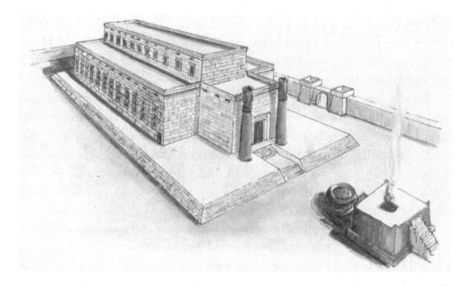

Solomon Temple

The first element seen in Isaiah's description of the Lord is his glory and immenseness. This manifestation of the Lord in his glory is eclipsed only by the mount of transfiguration and John's visions in the book of Revelation. When God grants such blessings, the obvious question becomes, how does the finite and feeble mind describe or stand in the presence of pure holiness and glory? What can any mere man conclude about God's glory after this, other than, he is holy and, "high and lifted up"!

The scene, no doubt, must have been terrifying, yet necessary in order to capture the heart, soul and mind of Isaiah! His view of God had to be corrected. There could be no doubt in his mind and heart of God's character! When God is compared to earthly kings, none can stand in his shadow! Isaiah must be drawn to the realization that in comparison to God, King Uzziah, his power, and all his accomplishments were nothing!

It is difficult, if not impossible to imagine how Isaiah must have felt looking at a throne that must have been beyond anything he had ever seen. Perhaps, our understanding can be helped somewhat, by imagining someone in a deep valley surrounded by towering mountains on all sides. The sense of awe at such magnificence is nothing less than breathtaking. When we see such glory, many instinctively worship and praise the one that created it all.

However, it is not just the throne that has Isaiah stricken with reverential awe, it is the person sitting on it; it is the Lord himself! He is the one, exalted, high and lifted. The throne only serves to reinforce and highlight this reality.

Finally, in describing the Lord, Isaiah declares, "His train filled the temple and smoke filled the room". Again, here is where communication breaks down. This is Isaiah's problem as his attention focus, not to the Lord's face or the throne, but the hem or train of the Lord sitting on the throne. As John could only struggle to find words to describe his beatific visions of heaven, so Isaiah could go no further than to say, "His train filled the Temple". (Oswalt, *The Book of Isaiah*, 178)

In other words, his glory filled every inch; every crevice, and every part of the Temple. This is the idea presented by the robe; the immenseness of God, that space cannot contain him! After seeing all this, I can only assume that Isaiah's response would be similar to any human being when in the presence of pure holiness—to fall prostrate before him, in utter fear and trembling!

THE CREATURE'S PROPER RESPONSE TO HOLINESS

To magnify his glory further, there were Seraphim, who were either standing or flying above the Lord. Two observations immediately stand out about these beings. First, though *holy* and perfect in every way, they covered themselves with their wings. Even in their splendor and sinlessness, they saw themselves as being unfit to look at God, who above all else is—holy!

The second fact about the Seraphim is, instead of falling prostrate before the LORD, Isaiah records that they worship him continuously. What a beautiful picture of the proper response of the creature when in the presence of God and his *holiness*; not just to be in awe (although we must), but filled with praise and worship!

The fourth and fifth chapters of the book of Revelation emphasize this fact even clearer, where John saw four beasts declaring the wondrous works of Jesus Christ and then bursting forth with praise and worship before him (Revelation 4:2, 5, 8-11). They gave all praise to God the Son because only he is worthy to receive "Blessing, and honor, and glory, and power", for his redemptive and creative work (Revelation 5:12, 13).

This seems to be the essence of the Seraphim's spontaneous and nonstop worship to the Lord in their chant, "holy, holy, holy, is the LORD of hosts: the whole earth is full of his glory" (Isaiah 6:3). Their actions and words are of vital importance to our understanding of God's nature. He does not just want Isaiah to see His glory, he wanted him to know who and what he is. Commenting on this phrase, Dr. Oswalt writes, "Here the cognitive and rational element is introduced, providing one more indication that revelation does not merely come through raw experience, but also through divinely given cognitive interpretation of that experience". (Oswalt, *The Book of Isaiah*, 180)

Like Moses, Isaiah's mission and message needed more than an experience. As stated earlier, God was sending him before a people who had continually violated his laws. Instead of being a light among the Gentile nations around them, they had taken on their practices. They were no longer holy, set apart and different. They had forgotten God's commands given to their forefather. They were to be *holy* and declare his name among the Gentiles; in their current state, that task was impossible.

Therefore, to restore them to a proper state of holiness, God revealed through the Seraphim's actions his *holiness*. In a sense, he was revealing the essence of his moral character. Without such knowledge, Isaiah might never come to understand that God is not just *holy*, he is, "holy, holy, holy", and "the Lord of hosts". If he did not understand this as God's messenger, he could not disclose it to God's people.

Many believe the threefold holy, or the *Trisagion*, is a reference to the Trinity. This could be the case, but the context does not seem to support such a conclusion. The focus is clearly the holiness and glory of God. Isaiah and any Jew would have understood the Seraphim's chant as the highest superlative. Therefore, it seems that the action of these beings stressed God's *holiness* above all else.

In fact, found in the words and actions of the Seraphim are excellent pictures of God's *holiness*. They properly show God's complete distinctiveness and separateness. There is none comparable to him in purity; majesty, power or splendor, he is God and there is none like him! That is the motivation behind the *Trisagion*, to emphasize God's *holiness*!

THE HOLINESS OF GOD LAY BARE MAN'S UTTER SINFULNESS

Once people confronts the *holiness* of God, they see themselves! Put another way, it is difficult for a person to see how much they need God without first knowing how holy he is and how corrupt they are. That is what happened to Isaiah, God's holiness revealed his wretchedness, vileness and unworthiness before him.

The only conclusion possible after realizing such hopelessness was to cry out, "Woe is me! for I am undone; because I am a man of unclean lips". This powerful word spoken by the prophet, not only emphasize his sinfulness, but his fear of seeing ". . . the King, the LORD of hosts" (Isaiah 6:5). Surely, in his mind, death was imminent!

The prophet gives two reasons for such a damning conclusion. First, he is a "man with unclean lips". He stresses unclean lips and not heart because the lips express the desire and thoughts of the heart (Romans 10:9). Isaiah knew that, unlike the beings surrounding the LORD's throne, his lips did not continuously sing the praises of God, not necessarily because he did not want to, but his evil heart would never allow it (Romans 7:21,23).

Second, he pronounces on himself the only sentence appropriate for his situation—woe! Once a person comes face-to-face with God, they see their own sinfulness and their utter defilement. He suddenly realized that not only were his lips unclean but his countrymen were in the same predicament. Their lips to, did not pour forth praises to God as they should have.

This is behind Isaiah's proclamation, "for I am undone", which literally means 'ruined' or 'perish'. For him, there was no future or hope! Most would have begged God for compassion and mercy at this point, or made some incredible oath if given another chance. However, Isaiah did none of these, the text seems to imply a willingness on his part to take whatever judgment God had for him.

God's Holiness Reveals Our Inability To Stand In His Presence

Though God knows man's natural hostility towards him, he still shows mercy and pity. What better example of this than the picture set before us of Isaiah amid God's *holiness*. He has no wings to protect his unholiness. Like Adam when confronted by God in his disobedience, he had no words of praise, only condemnation, guilt and shame. Isaiah needed and received God's mercy and grace through the burning coal taken from the altar and placed on his lips by one of the Seraphim (Isaiah 6:6).

Assuming the temple spoken of by Isaiah was Solomon's Temple (see image on page 5). the altar in question would have been the Altar of Burnt Offering located in the main court. This is significant because the fire on this altar burned continuously (Leviticus 6:12-15). Another important truth seen in the burning coals is the fact that, fire in the Bible is typical of purifying.

With this in mind, it becomes clear that God intends to teach us through Isaiah, that as sin separates us from him, so must his purifying fire purged it from us if we are to be united with him (Psalms 24:3-6). In his commentary on this chapter, Oswalt makes this point about the coal from the altar and its purifying affect, "When God takes away the iniquity and sin in which we have lived for years, the experience is a wrenching, searing one". Why? Because, it is the death of self, and the resurrection of a new creature altogether unlike the old one, with its superior self-sufficiency and outright hatred of God! This is the spirit residing in all unsaved people; it never gives up without a fight (Romans 7:18-23). In this regards, Oswalt writes, "Apart from the fires of self-surrender and divine surgery the clean heart is an impossibility". (Oswalt, *The Book of Isaiah*, 185)

Up to this point, the speakers had been the Seraphim and Isaiah, the Lord had remained silent. Scripture gives no reason for this, and therefore, it's pointless to speculate about why this was the case. But Isaiah and the Seraphim's response does reveal a remarkable truth about spiritual experiences. It suggests that such experiences are not an end in and of themselves. God does not give us a Mount Sinai (Exodus 3:3), a Damascus Road (Acts 9:3-6), or even a Mount Transfiguration experience (Matthew 17:1-6), just for a spiritual high. Such manifestation of God's glory instinctually brings the creature to the awareness of God's *holiness* and his worthiness to be worshipped and adored!

This is why Isaiah responded as he did to God's question of, "Whom shall I send, and who will go for us" (Isaiah 6:8)? Most theologians believe that this question was directed, "at the heavenly host, either visibly present or implied", and not Isaiah. (Oswalt, *The Book of Isaiah*, 185) But to the one who has come face-to-face with *holiness*, it does not matter. All that does matters is the tremendous need and desire to serve! So Isaiah spontaneously answers, "Here am I, send me"!

This is more than a casual response from someone responding to a solicitation for help. This is almost a plea steeped, not only in humility but unworthiness (Matthew 5:3, 8). It is as if though, after seeing what God had so graciously done to and for him, he asks, "though I am not worthy, will I do"? (Oswalt, *The Book of Isaiah*, 186)

Isaiah's experience was necessary in order to give him perspective of his own unworthiness because of his sin. His experience demonstrates to the church today that until she fully realize how holy God is and how vile and corrupt men are, all evangelistic efforts will be futile!

QUESTIONS TO PONDER

1. How does John 1:18 and John 12:41 help our understanding of the probable identity of the person sitting on the throne?
2. Though none of God's attributes are above the other, why is his holiness so prominent in the Bible?
3. Why is the holiness of God not emphasized today?
4. How does the holiness of God help our understanding of why He sent His Son into the world?
5. What did putting the coal on Isaiah's lip symbolized?
6. Though perfect beings, the Seraphim covered their eyes and feet. What does this say about how we should respond to God's holiness, especially in worship?

CHAPTER 2

What is Sin

"**A** man of unclean lips"! That was Isaiah's analysis of himself and his people after being in the presence of God's holiness! However, it was not the uncleanness of his lips that drove him to that conclusion, it was his understanding of his own *sinfulness*! In essence, *sin* is what makes us unholy and unable to stand in God's presence. Like Isaiah, we have become people who are 'undone' and incapable of doing the one thing God created us for—to be holy and glorify him! We hear much talk about *sin*, but rarely is the time taken to explain what it is, and its impact upon humanity. That is the goal of this chapter.

Having said that, let us look at *sin's* definition. Stated succinctly, *sin* is the lack of conformity to the moral law of God in deeds; disposition, and thought. In the Bible, *sin* is presented in different words and phrases. Some examples are as follows.

1. Missing the mark or the standard of God (Romans 3:23)
2. Transgression, or law breaking (First John 3:4)
3. Disobedience, with the idea of rebellion (Ephesians 2:2)
4. Abominations, which can be described as something morally disgusting to God, such as going through religious motion without sincerity (Ezekiel 20 and Isaiah 1:10-13)
5. Evil, which is described, as something morally lacking in terms of deeds, thoughts, words, and intentions; elements of sin include:

   1. Pride (Isaiah 14:3)
   2. Unbelief, unfaithfulness, disloyalty or a lack of trusting God (Genesis 3)
   3. Deception by Satan or others (Genesis 3:13)
   4. Self-righteousness or legalism

These expressions are stark contrasts to the holiness of God; yet without this contrast, it is difficult to fully see God's holiness. In other words, God's holiness is like the diamond set against the black cloth in a jewelry store. Though the diamond is beautiful in and of itself, it is the black cloth that brings out its beauty and splendor even more.

Though not perfect, this simple illustration gives us some idea of the chasm between God's holiness and *sin*. Regarding this chasm, Ralph Venning writes, ". . . sin is the dare of God's justice, the rape of his mercy, the jeer of his patience, the slight of his power, the contempt of his love". (Venning, Ralph, *The Sinfulness of Sin*. Edingburgh, Scotland: The Banner of Truth Trust, 1965, 32) In these next three chapters, we will look at what caused this rift, and the meaning and nature of *sin*. Hopefully, at the conclusion, the reader will have a better understanding of why *sin* totally separates man from God.

The curious reader might raise the question, "Why three chapters on sin"? The answer lies in the fact that once *sin* entered the world, it complicated everything. It complicated man's relationship with one another, to creation, to us as individuals, and finally it destroyed humanity's relationship to its Creator. All this combined with the misconception that *sin* is something abstract and independent of man's body and therefore, unrelated to his spiritual state warrants this level of attention.

In other words, to see *sin* for what it is, we first must remove its cloak of deception. To do so, we start off with this declarative statement about *sin*: it is a power, force or principle that is the antithesis of holiness, and is within every person that is born. (Barackman, William. *Practical Christian Theology, Examining the Great Doctrines of the Faith, Third Edition.* Grand Rapids, Michigan: Kregel, 1988, 290, 291) It controls every part of man's being: his mind, soul, heart, intellect, thoughts and conscience! *Sin* controls them all, it is their master; relentless, resolute, and controlling every aspect of their being! The Apostle Paul give this summation of sin's power over humanity, "For what I would, that do I not; but what I hate, that do I" (Romans 7:15). This is the state and condition of; not some of humanity, but all; enslaved to this dreadful and terrible power.

THE CAUSE OF MAN'S STATE

How did man come to this state? After all, God created him perfect and in his image and likeness; he was the pinnacle of his creation! As such,

God placed Adam in the Garden of Eden to rule, tend it, replenish the earth, and glorify him forever. This was God's will, not just for Adam, but the human race which he would generate. What changed it? How could such a perfect being, living in a pristine environment and lacking nothing; either physically or emotionally, choose to disobey God and in doing so, lose everything?

That's the age-old question and one that has haunted men and women throughout time. It haunts the husband, who loses everything for a one-night stand, or the businessperson caught embezzling the company's funds. Regardless of the crime or act, it's traceable to this single root cause—sin, and its inherent power over humanity! That's the reason behind people's troubles, regardless of the situation or person involved. Humanity must understand that the answers to all its problems are not within the pages or speeches of philosophers, psychologists or the halls of academia; but instead are given in God's Word—the Holy Bible! The Bible is the only source that explains the creation of our world; the universe, creation, and the origin and physiological makeup of the first man and woman. Only the Bible helps us know of man's original perfection and fellowship with God.

In man's original state at creation, there was perfect harmony between Adam, Eve, all animal life, nature, and God! However, all this changed once Adam listened to the words of his wife and ate from the tree forbidden by God (Genesis 1:6). Once he did that, he *sinned*, or trespassed against God and became a sinner!

Not only did he become a sinner, his nature changed from one of perfection to imperfection. As a result, he could no longer fellowship and walk with God! In the truest sense of the word, he along with all mankind suffered spiritual death or spiritual separation from God (Genesis 5:3)!

To better understand this statement and how God can justifiably hold every person accountable for the one act committed by Adam, two key facts must be understood about him. First, he was the federal head or representative head of all humanity. When he acted, he acted on behalf of us all. (Barackman, *Practical Theology*, 299, 300)

We see a convincing example of this in our form of government. When elected representatives are sent to Washington D.C. or our state capitols; they go on behalf of their constituents, who understands, that even though they play no active role in passing laws, their representatives' actions binds them to those laws. This same idea is behind the term federal head when referring to Adam; he acted for all of humanity; so that when he *sinned*, all of humanity *sinned* in him.

This leads to the Second fact: all of humanity was *seminally* present in Adam; regardless of race, creed or ethnicity! This should pose no problem since it's nothing more than the manifestation of like begetting like.

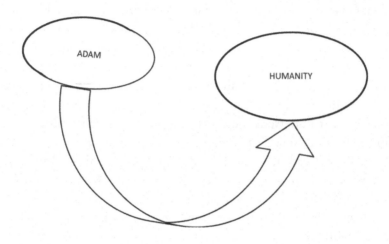

The Relationship Between Adam and Humanity

This clear and obvious fact should dispel the insidious concept of human beings descending or evolving from ape-like creatures. Adam was created as an ordinary man, having the same features and traits as modern humans and not some club-dragging half-man creature looking for his next meal.

How can any other reasonable conclusion be drawn after reading the first chapter of Genesis, which speaks of a being having the ability of communicating and fellowshipping with his Creator? This fact alone proves that intelligence; volition, emotions and moral capacity characterized the first man.

Otherwise, how could he handle the varied and complex responsibilities and duties associated with a caretaker? Add to these the responsibility of naming the animals; caring for the various plants and vegetation life, providing and caring for his wife, further supports the fact; Adam was a mature, rational person from the beginning, and perfect in every respect.

The Core Problem Of Humanity

What is man's basic problem? Is it not his lack of knowledge and acceptance of Adam's *sin* and its direct link to all of us? Admittedly, acknowledgment of this fact does bring with it the inescapable reality of recognizing God as creator. The former is not a problem for most; it is the latter that most people not only deny, but reject outright.

Why this blindness among humanity, especially when deep within the recesses of every soul, though not obvious to the natural mind, is a longing to worship God? This is not just a matter of dogma, but pure logic. What other explanation is there to explain the incessant desire of people to idolize objects; ourselves, and one another? Even worse, what drives people to drugs, alcohol, and other vices in order to seek happiness and peace? The reality, is that behind it all, is a spiritual deficiency within each soul seeking not a physical satisfaction, but one deeply spiritual.

Therefore, only as we understand Adam and the impact of his disobedience upon all of mankind will people see the real reason behind the problems that constantly haunts us. As stated earlier, Adam had perfect harmony and fellowship with God before he *sinned!* In that state, he experienced peace and tranquility, not just between himself, his wife and God, but even among the animals and nature.

Another reason for mentioning all this, is to highlight the fact that when God created Adam, he did something unique and extraordinary; he breathed into him the breath of life (Genesis 2:7). While it's understandable that God does not have physical eyes, legs or ears; in a way not revealed to us, he became more personable in the creation of Adam. In a sense, he breathed into him a part of himself. This means the life source of the first man, as well as every living being, is God himself! Though I cannot be dogmatic about this, I think this is one of the, if not the sole reason, that Adam was able to identify and commune with God.

But when Adam disobeyed God, his whole nature and being became corrupt by the *sin force* (discussed in a later chapter). His life source did not change, because it came from God. It remained as it always had, but because of the corruptness of his human nature brought about by *sin*, he could no longer identify with God. Again, the life received from God, that is 'God's breath', was not corrupt or defective, but his human nature now took on the nature or character of *sin*.

To illustrate this truth, let's look at a picture of water and a pack of cool-aid. In its natural state, water meets and satisfies people's thirst. However, once cool-aid powder is mixed with it, the properties of the cool-aid are so dominant that the water is no longer regarded as water, but cool-aid! Though still water, it no longer taste like water nor can it serve to fully satisfy a person's thirst. It is now cool-aid and cannot be reverted back to its original state. This crude illustration, though not perfect, helps us understand how sin permanently affected Adam's nature.

This terrible force within Adam made being in God's presence impossible. He was cut-off from him forever! He did not lose his life, but he suffered spiritual separation or spiritual death. Though the life of God remained and would always remain within him, it would never be able to express itself perfectly because it also had, in a sense, been cut-off from its source. The only way Adam could enjoy real life again would be to be reunited with his creator.

THE CONSEQUENCE OF ADAM'S DISOBEDIENCE

Adam's disobedience and its subsequent consequences did not end with him but passed on to his posterity. Therefore, his plight became humanity's for all time. In summary, the *sin force* is humanity's greatest enemy because it is the means that separates us from God!

Scripture helps us understand its power and influence over people and angelic beings by often personifying it. As human, living in a physical realm, this is perhaps the easiest way for the Spirit of God to make his truths intelligible to us, especially when talking about *sin*.

For example, consider these words in the first book of the Bible regarding Cain's condition prior to killing his brother, ". . . sin lieth at the door" (Genesis 4:7). This verse portrays the *sin force* as crouching like an animal, waiting to seize his prey, or in this case, the heart of Cain as it eventually did (Genesis 4:8). That is *sin's* power!

Also, in this expression, evil is not only portrayed in its purest form but also shown as being the governing principle of the *sin force*. Just as the Seraphim could speak of God as, "holy, holy, holy", when declaring his essential nature, so Scripture portrays the *sin force* as an entity that typify evil and the antithesis of God's holiness. It hates God and all he stands for and seeks only one thing, and one thing only—to "ungod God". (Ralph Venning, *The Sinfulness of Sin*, 31)

This explains why people in general blaspheme and mock God! Though they say they love Him, in fact, they hate and despises Him (Numbers 11:20; Acts 7:51; Romans 1:30), all because of the *sin force*!

If these only characterize historical figures such as; Hitler, Stalin, Saddam Hussein or even Osama Ben Laden; no one would object to these things accurately describing their nature. However, in question are not such men necessarily, but humankind as a whole; since the issue at hand is man's heart—a heart that is cold, evil, and dead. A heart the Bible declares as, ". . . deceitful above all things, and desperately wicked: who can know it" (Jeremiah 17:9).

Who among us could ever believe that within each of us lies the potential not only to do those deeds done by men such as Hitler and Hussein, but worse (Matthew 24:12)! The truth is, none of us know what we are capable of doing until situations or conditions present themselves. In a sense, 'sin lies' at each person's door waiting for an opportunity to unleash its power!

THE UNYIELDING POWER OF THE SIN FORCE

To humanity at large, all this talk about a sin force is foolishness because in the minds of men and women, they see themselves as being in perfect harmony with God. To them, he is not only a friend, but the best of friends; understanding of their ways, tolerant of their behavior and compromising in his laws. Such views of God are prime examples of how *sin* has blinded the mind of man's understanding as it relates to his nature and character.

As a result, the God who appeared to Moses and the Hebrew children at Mount Sinai with his strict requirements about how they were to approach him (Exodus 4:4-5; 19:10-12) is dismissed entirely. Even more inconceivable is a God so perfect in holiness, that his eyes are too pure to look upon evil, let alone approve of *sin* in any form (Habakkuk 1:13)! He is a God, who is perfectly just, wholly pure, and changeless in all his ways!

There is no compromise when it comes to God's standards and laws! As stated in the previous chapter, even poor Uzzah, who was struck dead for simply trying to prevent the Ark of the Covenant from falling into the mud (I Chronicle 13:9-10)! Though his intention was honorable and authentic; at stake was not his honor nor his sincerity, but the holiness of God! This is the God of the Holy Bible and the God *sin* desires to unseat.

Not only is *sin* a *force,* it reveals itself through people's actions. The Bible declares that anyone who, ". . . committeth sin transgresseth also the law: for sin is the transgression of the law" (I John 3:4). This is perhaps the simplest definition of, not what *sin* is, but what *sin* does; it, 'transgress the law' (emphasis added).

This is a fundamental spiritual truth; we must always distinguish the source from the act. It is the *sin force* working through our corrupt nature that produces the acts or 'transgressions of the law' which we call *sin* or sins.

The specific 'law' in view in I John 3:4 is God's Commandments. The other word in that same verse is transgress, which means to step over a fixed boundary. So the *sin force* compels a person to cross the boundaries set up by the Commandments of God. Not only does this apply to God's law, but laws set up by society, since God ordained and sanctioned them to maintain law and order in society (Romans 13:1-2).

The Law Energize Sin

This verse from the Apostle John's first letter (I John 3:4), reveals another notable feature of *sin*—it works with the law. Again, the Apostle Paul brings this out in the fifth chapter of his letter to the first-century

Christians living in Rome. Notice what he says, "but sin is not imputed when there is no law" (Romans 5:13). According to Barnes, the principle is clear "if there is no law, there can be no wrong, or transgression. (Albert Barnes, *Barnes' Notes,* Romans 5:12-21) In other words, "the strength of sin is the law", (I Corinthians 15:56)!

Again we see this truth expounded in the seventh chapter of the Apostle Paul's letter to the same Christians, starting at the eighth verse. Note his argument, "But sin, taking occasion by the commandment, wrought in me all manner of concupiscence, for, without the law sin was dead", (Romans 7:8).

The term 'occasion" carries the idea of 'opportunity'. Paul use this term to highlight the fact that the law of God, or any law for that matter, excites or fuel the *sin force*. Take, for example, the patch of grass a person has walked passed for years without being tempted to step on it. But once the owner places a sign that says, 'Do not walk on the grass'; suddenly this 'law' gives *sin* opportunity; it (the law) stirs up *sin* and in doing so; compels the person to walk on the grass!

The immediate conclusion by some might be that the law is evil or makes us *sin*. However, there could be nothing further from the truth. Notice Paul's statement again, "But sin, taking occasion by the commandment". The blame lies with the sin force; it is the culprit! It "wrought in me all manner of concupiscence or lust", not the law! The *sin force* is always behind evil, cloaked and working its diabolical schemes through the nature of humans and fallen angels.

Therefore, something is needed to reveal its true nature and purpose. That 'something' according to the Apostle Paul, is the law, "For without the law sin was dead". His argument is that, 'without the law' or where the law is not given, 'sin is dead'. Its power is gone, not broken. As showed by the sign on the grass, there is nothing to provoke or incite it.

THE EXTENT OF THE SIN FORCE'S POWER

Perhaps, the greatest question becomes: "If the facts presented in the previous section is true, how is it that Lucifer, a perfect being surrounded by other perfect beings in a perfect environment, sin"? What cause him to do so? It is clear that the *sin force* was not in Heaven. Any conclusion to the contrary borders on, if not outright stand, on the precipice of heresy, for it suggests Heaven; the dwelling place of the Most High God (I Kings

8:30, 39, 43; I Chronicles 6:21, 30-33), is a place where sin and holiness coexisted. It also challenge the nature of God's holiness and confirms the consensus of modern society that he is tolerant and overlooks sin after all. Taking a phrase from the Apostle Paul, "May it never be"!

So how are we to understand Lucifer's fall, since Scripture makes it abundantly clear that it resulted from his disobedience. This fact combined with the previous statements about *sin* and the law poses an even greater problem, "What law had God established in Heaven that Lucifer disobeyed"?

In other words, on the surface, it appears Lucifer's *sinned* apart from any law. If this hypothesis is true, the principle or law of sin becomes null and void (Romans. 5:13b). However, we know this not to be the case because Scripture affirms not only his disobedience and subsequent fall, but also the fall of those who followed his example. So the issue is not, did Lucifer disobey any law, since Scripture is clear on that point, as well as the result of his *sin* (Isaiah 14:12-14; cf. Revelation 12:9)! Instead, the real issue becomes what law did he violate?

The Spirit helps our understanding through these inspired words from the Apostle Paul, "For by him were all things created, that are in heaven, and that are in earth, visible and invisible, whether they be thrones, or dominions, or principalities, or powers: all things were created by him, and for him" (Colossians 1:16).

In that single passage, The Spirit of God gives the primary purpose of all creation: it is 'for him', that is, for service and praise to the Son of God. No passage in the Bible highlights this point more clearly than the fourth chapter of the book of Revelation. In that chapter, the Apostle John records that the heavenly host declares the Son of God as being the only one worthy to "receive glory and honour and power" (Revelation 4:11). Notice the reason given for this at the end of that same verse, "for thou hast created all things, and for thy pleasure they are and were created".

Here, is the key to understanding the nature of sin, and brings out Venning's earlier statement of its primary purpose—to "ungod God"! It cannot achieve that goal apart from willing vessels, yielding themselves over to its power. In this undertaking, it makes no distinction between angelic or human beings, perfect or imperfect, rich or poor; all are equally susceptible to its power and influence. This includes even Lucifer, though he was one of the most glorious and magnificent of all created beings (Ezekiel 28:12-14), he was not immune to its power and influence!

The Sin Force In Operation

How does the *sin force* overcome the will of rational beings and not only make them behave in a way they know to be wrong, but does so unhindered? The answer to this perplexing question is found in the New Testament letter written by James. In that letter, James tells us; this powerlessness start with a heart consumed with lust (James 1:14, 15). Here, is the main reason sin not only overcame Lucifer, but two other perfect beings; Adam and his wife Eve (discussed in the next chapter). It made them do what was unimaginable—rebel against their Creator.

Notice how James unfolds the drama and origin of sin in the fourteenth and fifteenth verse of the first chapter of his letter. First, he identifies the source of all *sin* as lust! To understand the importance of this term, we need to look at its definition.

Lust comes from a Greek word meaning, not just a longing, but a strong, intense and persistent desire. The idea behind this word is a relentless and restless desire within us that is awakened by some external Influence.

The Power of Lust

Here, lies the secret behind the power of lust; its relentlessness! It knows no boundaries, and will rules the heart that fails to recognize its ability. Three words in these verses are worth looking at because together they form the foundation upon which lust is built, as well as help us understand its intrinsic relationship to *sin* and the law. We must include 'law' in the equasion because it reveals the action to be sinful while at the same time fuels the *sin force* to act against it.

The Apostle Paul summarizes this in the seventh chapter of Romans this way, "I had not known that it was wrong to covet, if the law had not shown me", (Romans 7:7). The term covet in that passage come from the same Greek word translated as lust in the first chapter of James. The primary intent of this verse is not to single out the similarity between the two words, but rather to show that, without the law, there would be no knowledge of *sin*.

Also, key to understanding lust is to understand how the readers of James' letter understood its use. In other words, in the first-century, lust also had a positive meaning; as in the case when Jesus said, "With desire I have desired to eat this passover with you before I suffer" (Luke 22:15). Another example is Paul's words to the Christians in verse twenty-three of the first chapter of Philippians and the seventeen verse of First Thessalonians chapter two. All three passages use the same Greek word epithumia (Albert Barnes, *Barnes' Notes,* James 1:14) translated desire and spoken in a positively way.

However, in the James' passage under discussion, the Greek word used is negative and has an evil intent behind it. Albert Barnes writes that the normal thought behind this word is, ". . . some desire; some inclination; something which is unsatisfied now". (*Ibid*) That's the emphasis of lust here.

Having said that, let's return to the three terms in the verses from James that further brings out the meaning of lust. The first is "drawn away", which is a translation from a Greek word meaning 'to drag'. In their explanation of this verse, Jamieson, Fausset and Brown points out that the meaning behind this term is the idea of being, 'drawn away from truth and virtue', as such, it is always the beginning of temptation. (*JFB,* James 1:14)

This leads to the second word; 'of', which highlights the phrase 'drawn away'. In other words, it is not the external instrument or device (though they play a role) that drives any of us to *sin*, it's our own lust; our own desire that seeks to satisfy itself! That's what's brought out in this little word 'of', the drawing 'of our own lust'. Our own heart is the author!

That's where it all begins, and if stopped at that point, *sin* would never get a foothold!

This leads to the final word, 'enticed' which comes from a very intriguing Greek word. In explaining enticed, Albert Barnes offers this explanation, "caught; that is, he is seized by this power, and held fast". Barnes goes on to say, "he is led along and beguiled, until he falls into sin, as in a snare that springs suddenly upon him". (Albert Barnes, *Barnes' Notes,* James 1:14) At this point, the person is caught, and the beginnings of lust must now produce its evil fruit.

Again, the reader is reminded; lust does not necessarily lead to evil actions! For example, the craving for food is a legitimate and fundamental human need. However, when it drives a person to overeat, it then becomes evil. As stated earlier, lust in and of itself is not wrong because it is as much a part of our constitution as anything else. It only becomes evil when it controls either our thoughts, eating, or drinking.

This is James point in the passage under consideration; something forbidden and evil entered and seized the heart, resulting in *sin's* conception. This explains how a perfect being in a perfect environment, such as Lucifer, and even Adam, sinned. What was it that gave the *sin force* opportunity to exercise its destructive influence through Lucifer? What seized his heart and planted this seed of lust? Was it not pride? Was it not Lucifer's desire to be God? Was it not an overwhelming and a strong desire to receive the honor reserved only for God Himself? In essence was it not covetousness (Isaiah 14:13; cf. Ezekiel 28:6, 17)!

All these were sources of *sin's* inception in Lucifer's heart, brought about by a desire to go against the 'natural law' of heaven and earth where only God is worthy of worship (Colossians 1:16). Though I cannot be dogmatic, this is the law I believe Satan disobeyed!

However, because *sin* is an affront to and contrary to the nature of God, defiling and corrupting all that it touches; God not only expelled Lucifer from heaven, but all those who followed his example! He was a contaminant, that if left alone would have spread throughout the dwelling place of the Most Holy and Most High God!

Lucifer, whose name interestingly enough means 'morning star' (Isaiah 14:12) became Satan; the arch enemy of God and the accuser of all those who worship and serve him (Revelation 12:9). But as terrible as these acts were; the greatest and most damming result of Lucifer's rebellion was his eternal separation from God! This is the ultimate punishment of all who disobey God's commandments.

QUESTIONS TO CONSIDER

1. Why should sin be seen as a force?
2. How does this chapter better help you understand why a person's environment does not guarantee a person's outcome?
3. Why is it difficult to fully appreciate God's holiness if a person's concept of sin is different from what God says about it?
4. When you sin, do you ever consider any outside or internal forces at work?
5. How has this chapter help you better understand the power of lust and the danger it presents to all Christians?
6. How has this chapter help you better understand how to witness and counsel those who have difficulty with lust?
7. Read Galatians 5:16-18. What principle is given? How does the application of the principle enable the Christian to be victorious over lust, sin and ultimately the sin force?

CHAPTER 3

Adam and Eve and the Origin of Sin

Like Lucifer, *Adam's* role was to exalt and magnify God, not in heaven, but on earth! Created in the image of God, *Adam* was not only God's steward, he was his viceroy over all creation (Genesis 1:26). To complement and help him, God created woman, who *Adam* named *Eve* (Genesis 2).

Both were perfect beings in a perfect environment, lacking in nothing; either physically, mentally or emotionally, even their spiritual needs were met because they had fellowship and communion with God (Genesis 1:26-31). Their only duties were to take care of the garden and obey, not ten, but two commandments: replenish the earth and refrain from eating of the tree of the knowledge of good and evil (Genesis 1:22, 28; 2:17).

As stated in the previous chapter, because they possessed the spirit of God, there was perfect harmony. As 'He is holy', so were they! Disobedience or anything dishonoring to God never entered their mind.

ADAM AND EVE'S NATURE: PERFECT AND UNDEFILED

The only potential danger in the Garden of Eden was the possibility of this unity being broken. Without an external power entering them, there was nothing to cause them to rebel against their creator. Therefore, in order for their disposition towards God to change, a foreign power or influence, totally opposite of their nature had to be introduced into their environment. Remember, the law (God's commandments to *Adam and Eve*) was already there to provide guidelines and standards for *Adam and Eve* to keep their relationship with God.

Obeying God's commandments pleases and allows him to communicate and have fellowship with his people. Oddly enough, on the surface, it seems that as long as the sin force was missing or inoperative in the garden, *Adam and Eve* could keep the Law of God.

This almost contradicts Paul's statement that, "the strength of sin is the law" (I Corinthians 15:56b). In other words, as stated earlier, the point behind Paul's words was that the presence of any law gives power to, or energizes the sin force. However, any pristine environment suppresses or restricts it because there's nothing to awaken it. For example, the open gas line on a stove, whose fumes has permeated the entire house, will not explode until the smallest spark is introduced into that environment!

Though an extreme example, it portrays sin's potential in the heart of even a perfect being; regardless of whether angelic or human, whether living in heaven or the Garden of Eden. Both are equally susceptible to sin's absolute power once energized by the law. This is the reason *Adam and Eve* could walk past the Tree of the Knowledge of Good and Evil daily without eating from it, there was no compelling power to make them! Remember, *Adam and Eve's* nature was perfect and untainted by sin.

By nature, I mean that part of humanity that distinguishes us from animals and other life-forms. Paul alludes to this indirectly in the fifteenth chapter of First Corinthians when addressing the state of the resurrected body. He states in verse thirty-eight that "God giveth it a body as it hath pleased him, and to every seed his own body" (I Corinthians 15:38).

The similarity between what Paul said in First Corinthians and the current discussion about man's nature is this. A seed of wheat produces wheat instead of barley because of its inherent nature. That is because a "thing" is what it is because of its nature and acts based on that nature (cf. Matthew 7:16-20).

This is a fundamental principle and need no further explanation. So when talking about *Adam and Eve's* nature, what's in view is that entity within them that made them uniquely human beings and not animals. From their creation, their perfect nature made fellowship with God Possible (see image on next page).

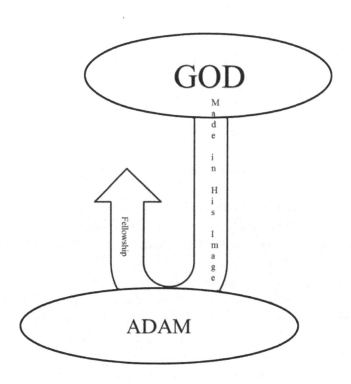

Man's Perfect Nature

This is the idea behind the earlier term, 'they were holy'; not in the same sense as God, but holy in the sense that their nature was perfect and undefiled. While the potential of sinning was there, it was not an integral part of their nature (remember the case involving the pitcher of water); otherwise God could not say, "everything that he had made . . . behold, it was very good", (Genesis 1:31). Essentially, their essence or nature was good because God created it that way!

Therefore, to sin or disobey God was just as much against their perfect and undefiled nature as it is for a fish to live out of water. Put another way, the governing principle of their nature was such that it could not sin, not because of their environment, but because of its constitution. So even though the law and opportunity was there, the inherent purity of their nature made sin powerless (see image on next page).

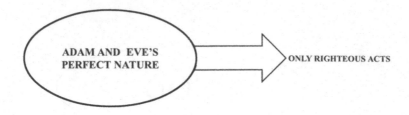

Adam and Eve's Perfect Nature

ADAM AND EVE'S UNTRIED INNOCENCE

Not only were the natures of *Adam and Eve* perfect, they were unacquainted with evil, both conceptually and experientially. Their state of innocence was of such that Scripture says of them that, ". . . they were both naked . . . and were not ashamed" (Genesis 2:25).

A good example (though imperfect), of their innocence and purity of heart is seen in the attitude of small children who are perfectly at ease playing together, regardless of race, creed or color. They are totally blinded to the inhibitions that hinders openness and honesty in human relationships.

The example of a child's innocence is not given to prove or disprove the argument of whether or not children are born in the same state of innocence as was *Adam and Eve* at creation. Instead, the example is given to shed light on how we are to understand the state of being that characterized the first human beings. They were innocent in the truest sense of the word! Though I cannot be dogmatic, their innocence would most likely have progressed naturally to its intended purpose, had the sin force not entered their world and contaminated their nature.

The other reason for the example of children's innocence was to highlight the fact that unlike children, who are gradually exposed to elements that affect their innocence, *Adam and Eve* were created as full grown adults. As such, the natural progression of maturity had not occurred; therefore, they were much more susceptible to temptation.

This conclusion about Adam and Eve is based on my own thinking and not an exact passage of Scripture in the Bible. However, I believe its validity can be proven to some extent by looking again at the example of small children. All of us know or know of adults who exhibits a childlike innocence either because of limited exposure to certain types of environments or over-protection by their parents. In a limited sense, such innocence can be said to be 'untried'.

However, none of those facts just mentioned can be applied to *Adam and Eve* because they had no parents, and as stated earlier, they were created fully grown. Additionally, their untried innocence had the greatest protection possible, God himself! With these facts in mind, one can easily see how they were said to be in a state of 'untried innocence'.

Because this was their condition, *Adam and Eve* responded and acted towards everything just like little children, innocently and without the least bit of inhibitions. Therefore, to alter their state negatively, an external force needed to invade both their environment and nature! That external force was sin; and just like the negative influences mentioned earlier that are brought against our young children daily with the express intent of stealing their innocence, so did the sin force rob *Adam and Eve's* innocence when it changed their nature from one of virtue to one of sin.

This fact regarding the importance of sin's impact on human nature cannot be overlooked. Our nature is the essence of our soul and governs everything about us! Therefore, it's only natural that this was the single part of *Adam and Eve* that sin attacked. But it did not stop at their soul, sin affected everything else about them; their heart, mind, thoughts, conscience and ultimately their innocence!

This fact regarding the impact sin has on the human nature is the sole reason why people cannot help but do evil acts. As pointed out earlier, the only reason *Adam and Eve* could produce pure and perfect deeds before being influence by sin was because their nature was pure. Likewise, *Adam and Eve* could only produce sinful acts after the sin force entered their nature because that now became their nature. As a result, their ability to produce virtuous deeds had become like the cool-aid, unable to revert to its original state! They were no longer holy beings, but sinners lacking any ability to do anything holy or righteous.

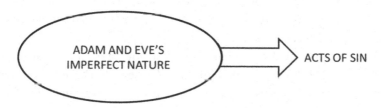

ADAM AND EVE'S IMPERFECT NATURE → ACTS OF SIN

The Principle of the Sin Nature

THE FIRST STAGE OF ADAM AND EVE'S FALL: THE DEVIL'S SUBTLETY

The previous sections of this chapter explored *Adam and Eve's* purpose, their original condition and relationship to God and how all those things changed. The closing section of this chapter continues this discussion by looking at the source behind their fall.

The focus up to this point has been the sin force and its impact on *Adam and Eve* and finally all of humanity. However, the sin force cannot work by itself; it needs, for lack of a better word, something or someone to activate it. As discussed in the previous chapter, the sin force lies passive until an opportunity presents itself. The problem in the Garden of Eden was its pristine state; sin was unknown, conceptually and factually!

In His infinite wisdom, God has chosen not to reveal to us sin's origin; just that it entered the human race through *Adam* (Romans 5:12). However, he does reveal to us how it became part of *Adam and Eve*. First, we learn that before the creation of the world, one of God's created beings in heaven named Lucifer had already rebelled against him (Isaiah 14:12-14; Revelation 12:3, 4). To reflect his rebellious nature, the Bible gives him the title of Satan or the Devil (Adversary and Accuser). To further emphasize his scheme and goal to unseat God, other names are assigned to him; such as tempter (Matthew 4:5); Beelzebub (Matthew 12:24); Enemy (Matthew 13:39); Evil One (Matthew 13:19); and many more (Revelation 12:3, 9; John 8:44).

The first place he's seen in Scripture however, is not the book of Isaiah or Ezekiel, but Genesis 3:1. There, he comes into contact with humans for the first time in a way most revealing of his deception, subtlety, and malicious intentions against God. In other words, Satan, or the Devil, approached *Eve* in a form that was attractive and innocent. This strategy of Satan was ideally suited to *Eve* in her state of untried innocence. What could be more harmless than what many believe to have been a snake? Again, like a child in their innocence, she never suspected the evil intentions behind its actions.

The description of the serpent, "more subtle than any beast of the field which the LORD God had made" (Genesis 3:1), reveals Satan's reasoning for choosing this particular creature—he was just like him; subtle, treacherous, and deceitful! Not only does it seems that the serpent was like Satan in nature, Scripture seem to indicate that like Satan before his fall, the serpent was superior to all the other beasts of the field.

The English Biblical Scholar of the eighteenth century John Gill writes that the meaning behind this verse is, he was, "made more subtle, that is, not naturally, but through Satan being in it, and using it in a remarkably subtle way, to answer his purposes, and gain his point". (John Gill, *John Gill's Exposition,* Genesis 3:1) Gill statement is not meant to reduce the serpent natural ability of subtlety, instead he wants to emphasize its heightened awareness because 'that old serpent, the Devil' (Revelation 12:9) had indwelt him!

Therefore, it is not surprising that Satan sought the most intelligent and cunning creature in paradise to strike at God's heart by deceiving and destroying the only being ever created in his own image—man! Note his approach and the simplicity and cunning behind his question. "Hast God indeed said, Ye shall not eat of every tree of the garden"? (Genesis 3:1) He does not ask just to get clarification from *Eve* about God's command about the tree. Instead, the real intent behind the question was to put a seed of doubt in the fertile soil of *Eve's* mind; a seed shrouded entirely in Satan's own deception and intense hatred of God.

The Second Stage of Adam and Eve's Fall: Satan's Distortion of God's Law

The question asked by many is, "How did Satan know that God had forbidden *Adam and Eve* to eat from the Tree of the Knowledge of Good and Evil? It seems unlikely that he was present when God gave the commandment to *Adam*, since God's declaration after each creative act was, 'it was very good'. In either case, the issue is not so much his knowledge of the command as it is his willingness to distort and use it to his own evil advantage.

Satan's willingness to distort God's Word is among his greatest weapon against God's people. He has no shame and will utilize this method whenever it benefits his cause; all one need do is remember his blatant and shameless distortion of God's Word when tempting Jesus Christ (Matthew 4:3-11). If he would dare approach the Son of God in that fashion, how much more so would he unhesitatingly unleash this weapon against mere finite human beings?

This is one of Satan's trump cards whose success is seen throughout many churches today. Why is distorting God's Word so powerful? The answer is obvious, what better way to get at man than by attacking his mind; the part of his being that govern his thoughts, his will, his beliefs, and ultimately his whole idea of God. This was the Devil's strategy in the Garden of Eden; to take God's crown jewel and bring him to disobey one of the only restrictions placed on him in that perfect place called 'Eden'. Satan knows and understands God's holy character more clearly than any created being! Furthermore, he understands and fully believed that once *Adam* disobeyed God, he would become as he was—condemned and separated from him forever, or so he thought.

Another intriguing question pondered by many is, "How was the serpent enabled to speak"? Though man have offered their theories as to how this did or did not happen, such speculations are unwarranted here as they lend nothing of value to the present discussion. The reality is, the Scriptural account simply declares, "And he said unto the woman", (Genesis 3:1b). Like the account of Creation, the facts are stated, "And God said", (Genesis 1:1-11, 20, 22, 26, 29) that is it! Nothing further need be said. The encounter between the devil and *Eve* is a statement of fact: there was the woman, there was the serpent, and he spoke to the woman. God the Spirit in his wisdom, chose not to give us answers to such questions as; why and how the serpent was enabled to speak, or what it looked like. Therefore, it is ridiculous and useless to speculate about such matters.

Having made that statement, let's look further at Satan's encounter with *Eve*. One thing for sure, the serpent's ability to talk to *Eve* must have aroused her attention and curiosity, instigating or urging her closer towards sin. Another interesting question about this encounter is the lack of *Adam's* response during the entire conversation. One reason for *Adam's* lack of response or intervention might be attributable to their state of innocence. Though they were perfect, they did not know everything perfectly then or ever. This is something only true of the omniscience God.

We see *Eve's* lack of knowledge in the first question posed to her. Notice the subtlety in Satan's question, filled with irreverence; sarcasm, arrogance, and pride, 'Hath God said'? Right away, he targets her innocence. Up to that point, the only beings she had known was God and *Adam*; and like a child, she trusted both implicitly. (Evans, Anthony T. *Spiritual Warfare*,

Renaissance Productions Inc. Cassette, 1991) But now, this intruder's innocent question becomes the slightest and smallest wedge between that trust.

As stated earlier, he used this same strategy when tempting Jesus Christ in the wilderness (Matthew 4:3-10), and continues do so now. He does not change, always coming off as, "trusting, unsuspecting, and seemingly looking out for our best interest". (Evans, *Warfare*) While, in fact, all along he is scheming and planting the same seed of doubt in our head as he did with Eve, 'Did God actually say that?'

If only Eve recognized, not that the serpent was talking (though that was important) but his questioning her creator's character and integrity. The reason an alarm did not sound in her heart was because the devil kept her focus on her desires and used them as the means of convincing her to disobey God! (Evans, *Warfare*)

Next, when comparing Genesis 2:17 with Genesis 3:4, we see the Devil directly contradicting God's Word. In the former, God told *Adam and Eve* they would surely die if they ate from the Tree of the Knowledge of Good and Evil. But in verse four of chapter three, the serpent says, "Ye shall not surely die". In this statement, the devil eliminates the consequence and punishment of eating from the tree. In doing so, he twisted God's Word, and in the process planted a seed in *Eve's* heart regarding God's trustworthiness.

At this point, the devil had started the process of removing God from the picture. She could not comprehend his deception, nor did she fully comprehend the danger before her. Before she knew it, the devil had convinced her that God was wrong in forbidding her and her husband from eating from the tree, and 'she did eat'. (Evans, *Warfare*)

THE THIRD STAGE OF ADAM AND EVE'S FALL: DECEPTION

In the New Testament book of First Corinthians, Paul makes this statement, 'The devil beguiled Eve'. The Greek word for beguile carries the idea of putting a piece of meat in a trap to catch an unsuspecting animal. Is this not a true picture of what happened to *Eve*? Satan used the exact law given by God as a snare causing Adam and Eve to sin.

Here, is where choice comes in because even though *Eve* was in a state of innocence, she had enough information to choose between ignoring or yielding to the devil's suggestion. She already knew of God's faithfulness and goodness. This fact, in conjunction with her perfect state, should have made it easier for her to make the right decision.

But notice what happened, ". . . the woman saw that the tree had fruit that was good to eat, nice to look at, and desirable for making someone wise" (Genesis 3:6, GW). Had this not occurred to her before? Had she not noticed the fruit before? What changed her disposition? Not the tree or the fruit, but something new to her, something called lust. This strange feeling she had never experienced before, not because it was not there, but because it laid dormant, waiting to be aroused.

Again, in the seventh chapter of Romans, the Apostle Paul helps us understand what's going on, "But sin took the opportunity provided by this commandment and made me have all kinds of wrong desires" (Romans 7:8, GW). Do you see the influence of the law energizing the sin force? The desire to eat is valuable because it is needed to keep us from starving. What was evil and wrong was disobeying the Law forbidding them to eat from the Tree of the Knowledge of Good and Evil. Satan says, "God knows that when you eat it your eyes will be opened. You will be like God, knowing good and evil" (Genesis 3:5, GW). Regarding this statement, Dr. Evans points out that, in this instance, "Satan attacks the righteousness of God by implying he is denying something good from them". (Evans, *Warfare*)

Why did *Eve* finally eat the fruit? Because the law had empowered the sin force! As a result, her heart and mind had become powerless to exercise her will to make the right choice. Perhaps, she still had reservations about disobeying God, but the desire for the fruit was overwhelming. Paul calls this, 'the motions (passions) of sins' (Romans 7:8), and here is the key phrase of that verse, "which were by the law, did work in our members to bring forth fruit unto death" (Romans 7:8).

Paul is not saying the law caused the act of disobedience, just that it became an accelerant to an already tense situation! As a result, the law becomes less resistible and sin more appealing, and subsequently *Eve* is 'drawn away of her own lust' (James 1:14). The devil's reprehensible plan had worked.

Being enticed, *Eve* took the bait and the devil had almost achieved his goal. I say almost only because the authority had been given to *Adam*, not *Eve*. As long as *Adam* did not eat from the tree, Satan's success would have been negligible and inconsequential.

Unfortunately, *Adam*, who apparently was with *Eve*, had watched all this! He had the power to overcome the devil and could have done so by saying two basic words—God Said! Instead, he took the fruit from *Eve* and 'he did eat' (Genesis 3:6).

As stated in the previous chapter, because *Adam* was the *Federal Head* of humanity, he acted on behalf of us all. Therefore, his actions, not only sentenced him to spiritual death, but all of humanity with him. In the fifth chapter of Paul's letter to the Christians at Rome, he sums this up in these words, ". . . as by one man sin entered into the world, and death by sin; and so death passed upon all men, for that all have sinned" (Romans 5:12).

This then marks the beginning of sin and its operation in the world through humanity. *Adam's* one act of disobedience brought the sin force into his nature. As a result, it changed his nature from one of holiness into one like itself—sin! It now became his master and rules through his nature.

Since he is our *Federal Head*, his actions became ours. Even more importantly, because all of humanity descends from *Adam*, we inherit his nature; no longer perfect, no longer pure, no longer undefiled, but tainted and corrupted by the sin force (Genesis 5:3). That nature now rules in all of us as it did *Adam and Eve*.

As stated earlier, it makes men and women, boys and girls, young and old, do all kinds of evil acts. Like an apple tree that will always produce apples because of its nature; so every man and woman, every boy and girl outside the saving power of Jesus Christ can only produce sinful unthinkable acts of evil. It is our nature!

QUESTIONS TO PONDER

1. What valuable lessons are learned about Satan's character from his first encounter with humanity?
2. What immediate danger is faced by the Christian who talks to Satan? Is there ever a time when a Christian should engage in a conversation with Satan? If yes, when and explain how. Can you provide Scriptural example?
3. How would you use James 1:13-14 to explain the steps involved in Satan's victory over Eve?

CHAPTER 4

Sin's Effect on Human Nature

"Wherefore, as by one man sin entered into the world, and death by sin; and so death passed upon all men, for that all have sinned" (Romans 5:12). This single verse from the New Testament Book of Romans summarizes the sole source of evil in the world. Though passages such as Psalms fifty-one and the seventeenth chapter of Jeremiah talks about the results and root of *sin*, neither are as accurate and complete as this passage of Scripture.

For example, in Psalms 51:5, David based his grief and subsequent repentance for sinning against God on the realization of the fact that he, "was shapen in iniquity; and in sin did my mother conceive me". At the heart of David's statement is not so much the truth involving his parents' condition as it is his own at conception.

This crucial difference highlight David's explanation for his transgression against the law of God as being, he 'was shaped' in that way. In his commentary on this verse, Albert Barnes emphasize the word shaped does not include the idea of being formed or molded. Instead, the thought is, though he does not know how, ". . . his sin could be traced back to his very birth"; that it was so deep and aggravated, that ". . . he could express his sense of it in no other way, than by saying that he was born a sinner". (Albert Barnes, *Barnes' Notes,* Psalm 51:5)Though David did not understand the cause of his *sin*, he recognized that somehow his own depravity was behind it. The same thing can be said about Jeremiah 17: 5-8. The Lord's words through the prophet Jeremiah regarding the wicked and deceitful nature of the human heart was directed at the nation of Israel and her idolatrous and evil ways.

Such condemning words from God might be justified and understandable if directed towards people who did not know him, but these were Israelites—God's people! They were chosen by him, protected by him; in essence their whole identity as a nation was due solely to God's grace. The only requirement charged to them was simply to obey his commandments and statues, and they would live prosperously in the land. Yet, their history shows they failed at every turn, not so much because they did not want to please God, but because of a corrupt and *deceitful* heart controlled by their *sin nature*.

SIN: THE CAUSE OF ALL EVIL

Sin is mankind's greatest enemy! The only hope of defeating it is to come to the same consciousness that David did; mainly that people are, 'shaped in iniquity'. In a sense, we come into the world walking backwards as it were, always regressing and never progressing! This is the only rational explanation for evil's rapid progression in the world.

Though the question of 'why' is often asked, the answer remains elusive because people refuse to seek the only source that has the answer—God's Word (Ephesians 4:17-19)! As a result, like blind men, they stumble here and there, trying this and that solution in an attempt to resolve the world's problems. The intent of this final chapter on *sin* is to look at why it is the source of all evil.

The first principle to remember is that sin entered the world through one man—Adam! As stated in the previous chapter, while Eve was the first to disobey God, she could not act on behalf of humanity because she was not its federal head. Therefore, Scripture makes it clear; *sin* did not enter the world through her, but through Adam (Romans 5:12). Though I cannot be dogmatic about this, I suppose if Adam had not yielded to Eve's invitation to eat the fruit, the world might have remained in its pristine state.

Paul's use of the term *sin* in Romans 5:12 is a reference to the source, not the act. In other words, Adam's transgression (disobedience) of God's Commandment was the direct result of the *sin force*, or principle, *entering* paradise through the devil! The verb used by Paul in this verse for entered literally means invaded. Doctor Martyn Lloyd-Jones in his commentary on this verse writes, "The Apostle does not mean that 'it began to be', but it 'entered in', it 'invaded' the world. *Sin* broke in; it intruded into man's life". (Lloyd-Jones, D. M. *Romans, An Exposition of Chapter 5: Assurance.* Grand Rapids, Michigan: Zondervan Publishing House, 1971, 194)

Paul personification of *sin* in Romans 5:12 not only highlight its power but its actuality! This is where many, including some Christians go

37

wrong; they fail to believe in *sin's* mighty power. Once it enters a world, or a person; it destroys and take its subject into full captivity, even if that world is perfect in every aspect. This is what happened to Adam and Eve; they became victims to the devil's subtlety and cunning. In doing so, they (Adam in particular) granted *sin* access to the world; condemning themselves and humanity!

HOW SIN WORKS IN US

The previous chapter focused on humanity's nature, or that entity, that makes man uniquely human. Its design was to highlight the fact that everything is governed by its nature. A fish lives in water because that is its *nature*. Birds fly and mammals can survive on land as well as in the water, again, all because of their nature. (Pentecost, Dwight W. *Things That Become Sound Doctrine*. Grand Rapids, Michigan: Kregel Publication, 1975, 13)

However, the part of humanity that distinguishes one person from another is not their *nature*, but that part of their nature called the *personality*, or *personhood*. Although an integral part of a person's *nature*, the *personality* is distinguished from our *nature* because it is the part of each human being that is regarded as the source of individuality; and identified by the personal pronoun "I". (Barackman. *Practical Christian Theology*, 258-259) Additionally, it is the one part of humanity that separates humans from animals.

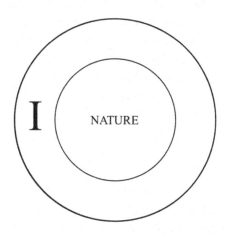

The "I" of Personhood

While it might appear that some members of the animal, primate and mammal family possess *personhood*, the reality is that when you think about it rationally, they do not! The greatest evidence of this is found in the very definition of what *personhood* is: *self-awareness, responsible moral self-determination*, and *unique self-expression*. (Barackman, *Practical Christian Theology*, 259) These attributes are what makes it possible for people to relate to each other; live together, act rationally, and make moral choices.

Furthermore, they also characterize God himself and therefore, help us understand the reason why the Bible only speaks of Adam and Eve being made in the image of God. Not that God looked like them, or any human being for that matter, but that people are endowed with those attributes of God that are transferable; such as love, compassion, mercy, anger, and pity.

Having said that, let us look briefly at the qualities that make up *personhood*. First, there is *self-awareness*. This quality in humanity makes it possible for beings, including angels, to know they are different from another person or thing (Barackman, *Practical Christian Theology*, 259).

Self-awareness goes beyond being aware of physical distinctions, such as skin color; hair color, gender, and so forth; it goes to the very core of the human psyche, unseen by the natural eye! In other words, each of us knows intuitively that he or she is their 'own self' and entirely different from anyone else. This is something every person is aware of; that they are human, or male or female; even that they are an Archangel and not Satan (cf. Jude 1:9); these are some of the cognizant facts behind 'self-awareness'.

The second aspect of *personhood* is *responsible moral self-determination*. This feature means that as a person develops, certain things are learned from his or her environment through parental guidance; education, friendship, experiences and so forth, which when combined with *self-awareness*, enables them to not only make moral choices, but held responsible for their actions.

When children are allowed to raise themselves apart from little or no supervision and training from their parents, this part of humanity suffers. In other words, when people are not held responsible and accountable for their actions, society becomes unruly because every person will resort to doing what is right in their own eyes.

These two aspects of personhood; self-awareness and *responsible moral self-determination*, naturally manifest themselves through each person's *unique self-expression*. This third aspect of *personhood, unique self-expression* is the most significant, as it highlights people's ability to express one's own self-awareness and responsible *moral self-determination*.

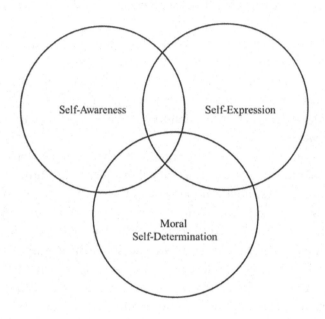

The Parts of Personhood

As stated earlier, *personhood* is part of one's *nature*. Understanding this fact helps us better understand the *sin force*. Though they are inseparable and dependent upon each other, the controlling entity is the *human nature,* because it dictates, controls and influence *personhood.* Therefore, an individual's *unique self-expression* is more than the outward appearance of *moral responsible self-determination* and *self-awareness,* it is a reflection of their nature.

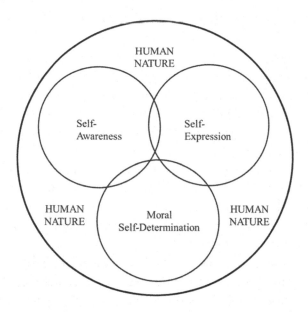

Personhood and Human Nature

As demonstrated by the image above, the *human nature* works in and through *personhood*. For example, a thief may be a loving father, a devoted friend or even a model citizen. From a moral stance, he knows and agrees stealing is wrong, he may even have enough *self-awareness* to know he is doing something he hates; yet, despite these facts, he still commits acts of burglary and theft. What is the key to understanding his actions? The Apostle Paul provides the answer in the seventh chapter of Romans as, "It is no longer I, but sin that dwells in me".

It is not 'I', the person or one's personhood, but the sin force that has become the dominant part of one's nature, 'working through their members'. That is why people sin, not necessarily because they want to, but because within them lives a force that not just influences them, but controls them through their nature and in the end through their personhood. The intent of this statement is not to condone evil; but provide the reason why it is so natural to us.

This brief discussion on personhood was necessary to add clarity to the concept of our human nature and its relationship to sin. An improper understanding of *personhood* makes it difficult to understand the biblical teaching of *sin* and its dominance over humanity.

THE EXTENT OF SIN'S POWER IN THOSE WHO ARE IN CHRIST

Any attempt to understand sin's power over all mankind must start with a proper understanding of the fifth chapter of Romans, especially verses 12 through 21. Prior to this passage, Paul had focused on the benefits of being justified (discussed later) by Christ (Romans 5:1-5). Having done that, he closes his argument by stressing the centrality of Christ and his redemptive work as the sole means of justification in verses 7 through 11.

Dr. Martyn Lloyd-Jones stress that verse 10 is the key verse of that passage and provides the reason why Paul began Romans 5:12 as he did. Notice what verse 10 says, "For if, when we were enemies, we were reconciled to God by the death of his Son, much more, being reconciled, we shall be saved by his life".

In his comments on this verse, Dr. Lloyd-Jones emphasize that Paul did not use the word 'by' at the end of this verse, but 'in' and is so translated in the Revised Version. In making this statement, Dr. Lloyd-Jones draws our attention to the fact that there exists an, ". . . intimate connection between Christ and ourselves". He further writes, "We are not being saved 'by' His life, we are being saved 'in' His life. (Lloyd-Jones, *Romans 5,* 174)

Paul's emphasis has to do with our realm of existence. As it relates to Christians, this realm emphasizes the fact that we are who we are, because of our intimate connection to Christ; we are a part of him! To help us understand this relationship, Jesus used the analogy of the vine and its branches (John 15), and Paul used the analogy of the body (I Corinthians 12). Both were used to highlight, not just a union, but the fact that all Christians are part of the body of Christ.

Paul goes one step further by declaring that, "I am crucified with Christ: nevertheless I live; yet not I, but Christ liveth in me . . ." (Galatian 2:20). What is it that distinguishes Christianity from religion? Is it not this mysterious relationship that Paul talks about here in Galatians, living, yet not living because the life he lives is not his own, but that of Jesus Christ! This is Paul's emphasis in the first eleven verses of the fifth chapter of Romans; to point out that our justification is made possible by our faith in Jesus Christ and the life he gives to Christians.

Realizing the reality of our relationship to Christ and the power that comes along with that relationship (Romans 5:10) helps us better understand Romans 5:12. In other words, we are saved solely because we are in Christ and nothing else! As Jesus declared in the gospel of John, he is the source of our existence; without him, Christians can do nothing (John 15:4-5)! Paul's argument in Romans 5:10 is, that is who we are now. But before we were saved 'in' Christ, Romans 5:12 tell us that we were 'in' Adam! Just as we are now 'saved in' Christ, or better yet; just as we have been declared justified or declared righteous with God because of our relationship to him, so God condemned all humanity because of its relationship to Adam!

THE EXTENT OF SIN'S POWER IN THOSE WHO ARE IN ADAM

The previous section's goal was to introduce the reader to the significance of the spiritual relationship between Christians and Jesus Christ. The goal was to emphasize that Christians are who they are because of their union with Jesus Christ, and not because of anything inherent in their nature.

The other purpose was to help our understanding of the relationship between Adam and all of humanity. This is Paul's emphasis in Romans 5:12; to draw a distinction between who Christians are because of their union with Jesus Christ (Romans 5:9, 10), and who man is because of his union with Adam. Both relationships are based on the fact that both groups are 'in' their respective head; the Christian is 'saved in' Christ and the rest of humanity is judged and condemned 'in' Adam (cf. Romans 5:18)!

Note Paul's statement regarding humanity's relationship to Adam in Romans 5:12, "Wherefore, as by one man sin entered into the world". *Sin* in this passage has to do, not with the act, but the source itself! Sinful acts are not the results of a defect in character, or an unhealthy environment, but the result of the *sin force* that entered in through Adam (Lloyd-Jones, *Romans 5*, 199).

As stated earlier, when the *sin force* entered Adam, it became the dominating principle or force in his *nature* causing him to act, not in a manner that was perfect and good, but *sinful* and evil! Paul's argument is, since all humanity was in Adam (that is, all people comes from Adam's seed), God declares that through Adam, ". . . all sinned"! This means, God not only hold Adam guilty of his *sin*, but all humanity because, as stated earlier, we were all seminally present in him when he *sinned* (Pentecost, *Sound Doctrine*, 14). To help our understanding of the *sin force's* power over Adam, we need to look back at our discussion on *personhood*. In that section, it was stressed that personhood, which is part of our human nature, is the medium by which the *sin force* works through.

Additionally, we talked briefly about the fact that also residing within our *nature* are 'the motions', or our *desires*. During that discussion, the emphasis was made that these *desires* in and of themselves are not evil, but good and necessary. However, when we let them control us, they are no longer functioning the way God designed them. In other words, Adam's desire to eat was an essential function given to him by God and therefore, good in and of itself; since failure to do so would have eventually deprived his body of essential nutrients needed to live. So obviously, simply eating was not Adam's *sin*; instead it was a failure to control his desire to eat from the forbidden tree. The result of his failure was twofold: *sin's* conception (James 1:15), and the corruption of his nature.

Again, though *personhood* and the *human nature* is one entity, the *nature* is the controlling agent. This reality means that every aspect of Adam's *personhood*, his mind, his will, his emotions and his *desires,* were now under the total control of this new force called *sin* which had now invaded and controlled his holy *nature*!

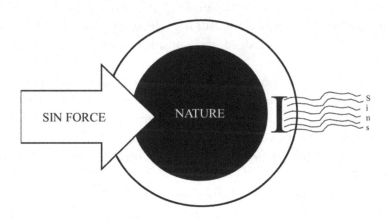

The Effects of the Sin Nature on Personhood

Not only did the *sin force* become the controlling force of Adam's *nature*, it also became the controlling force of his posterity. This brings us back to the Christian's relationship with Jesus Christ, and the life enjoyed because of that relationship. That relationship is parallel in this sense; just as all Christians are 'in' and therefore, live through Christ; so all of humanity (even Christians before being saved) is 'in' Adam because from his seed descended the human race.

UNDERSTANDING SPIRITUAL DEATH AND ITS RELATIONSHIP TO SIN

The radical change brought about in Adam's *nature* by the sin force not only destroyed its perfection, it became so much a part of his *nature* that he could no longer be regarded as perfect, but a *sinner!* In this new state, he became unholy, defiled, wicked and *depraved.*

As a result of this change, what could this new *nature* in Adam produce? Could it serve God or long for the sweet communion with its creator? Could it even look upon itself without shame and pity? The answer to all those questions is an unequivocally no! Because of his *nature*, Adam became something totally opposite of his Creator. In listening to his wife (who had listened to Satan), he had reached a point of no return. Consequently, he suffered the penalty of his disobedience; spiritual separation from God, or what is referred to in theology as *spiritual death!*

We often hear the term *spiritual death* used among Christians when talking to non-Christians. However, it is sometime difficult to explain its meaning and how it relates to the state of man. Therefore, to avoid confusion, I will attempt to explain it by first looking at the common understanding of the term death from a human perspective. In other words, everyone understands physical death because of its commonality among human beings as a whole. Therefore, what better analogy to use in explaining the biblical teaching of *spiritual death*?

First, note the obvious truth about physical death, it involves a dead body. When anyone touches a body lying in a casket, the one undeniable fact is the reality of its lifelessness. In essence, it is void of life and energy and not much more than a cold, stiff, hard shell. Though an extreme example, it aptly portrays the man or woman who is *spiritually dead.* Though physically alive, they are walking corpses; because like Adam, they are powerless to do the one thing they were created for; to live, fellowship with, and glorify God!

Before Jesus' crucifixion, he prayed for his disciples in the Garden of Gethsemane. The seventeenth chapter of the Gospel of John records this prayer. In the third verse of that chapter, we find these words, "And this is life eternal, that they might know thee the only true God, and Jesus Christ, whom thou hast sent". The significant part of that verse is the expression, "And this is life eternal, that they might know thee the only true God". Life then, according to Jesus involves knowing the 'only true God'. By implication, anyone who does not know God is not alive from a spiritual perspective.

Why is this relevant and what is its relationship to *spiritual death*? Too often, people associate life with just breathing and walking around. No doubt, that is living, but it is not life. According to Jesus, the quality of life is not measured in length of days, but whether one knows God.

Another crucial factor stated by Jesus in this verse about eternal life is brought out in his use of the word know. The Greek word translated as know in his prayer does not have in mind a casual acquaintance but the knowledge gained through experience and intimate fellowship; it has to do with relationship! Such knowledge of God is only possible after coming into the knowledge of his Son Jesus Christ (Hebrews 1:1-3), who revealed to mankind God the Father through deeds done in his life, suffering and death. Clearly then, Jesus' declaration is that eternal life is rooted in having a relationship with God. That's real life!

Adam knew this life and enjoyed it, up to the point when he disobeyed God! At that moment, his fellowship with God ceased. He lost his life, not because he died physically, but because his *nature* changed from one of perfection to one of corruption because of the *sin force*!

Since God is holy, and cannot be in the presence of *sin*, the harmony that existed between him and Adam at creation was no longer possible once the *sin force* entered him. As a result of *sin* in Adam, a separation occurred between him and God. Fellowship, communion and a relationship of any kind were no longer possible. In this sense, he was dead, again, not physically, but spiritually he was dead because he became separated from God!

SPIRITUAL DEATH AND HUMANITY

Spiritual death is tragic, not only because it separates people from their Creator, but it leads to sickness, hatred between people, all sorts of diseases, aging, and finally physical death,. These maladies comprise the second reality of *spiritual death* and are sometimes referred to as the teaching of, *original sin*; because they, along with God's judgment, condemnation and wrath, are the result of Adam's disobedience. These fundamental truths about *original sin* are emphasized to highlight the fact that its focus is not only on the first *sin* committed, but the consequences of that *sin* upon all humankind. Dr. Lloyd-Jones summarized *original* sin as the teaching ". . . that we are all guilty and held guilty in God's sight for the sin of Adam". (Lloyd-Jones, *Romans 5*, 211)

The third truth about physical death is that, they are cut-off from the living. In other words, there is a realm suited for the dead and another suited for the living. Both are designed to accommodate a particular state of existence. Just as this principle is true of the physical dead, so it is with those who are *spiritually dead.*

Both facts are designed to emphasize the truth, though not obvious to the naked eye, that coexisting in the physical world are two realms. One is spiritual; unseen and occupied by those possessing eternal life, while the other is physical and visible; and occupied by those *spiritually dead.* This is another way of identifying those who are saved 'in' Christ (spiritual realm), and those who are judged and condemned 'in' Adam (physical realm). The Bible goes even further in identifying the realm of those who are *spiritually dead* by using such terms as; the world and the kingdom of darkness. On the other hand, those having eternal life are identified as those who comprise the Kingdom of God; or the kingdom of Heaven.

Furthermore, the Bible uses specific terms to identify the inhabitants of the physical and spiritual realms. For example, when talking about those in the physical realm, such terms as; the children of disobedience, sinners, children of Satan, and children of wrath, are but a few used of those in the physical realm. Note the striking contrast to the terms associated with those living in the spiritual realm; saints, children of God, joint-heirs with Christ, salt, light, and children of light.

Another important fact about these two realms is; a person's behavior, attitude, and thinking; identify their realm. For example, our Lord Jesus Christ gives us a picture of those who are alive and part of the spiritual realm. Listen to His words on the Mount of Olives in Matthew chapters 5 to 7 as he describes them: poor, meek in spirit, peacemakers, merciful, hunger and thirsting after righteousness (Matthew 5:3-11). They are persecuted because of their identity and who they represent. Though not exhaustive, these are some identifying traits of those who are alive and constitute the Kingdom of Heaven, or what is sometimes referred to in Scripture as the Kingdom of God.

In the same way, Scripture paints a dire and gloomy portrait of the *spiritually dead* in the third chapter of Paul's letter to the Romans. In the eleventh verse of that chapter, he begins by describing them as unrighteous, unwise, and haters of God. If their lives were to be summed up in one statement, it is, they all continue to go wrong; not one of them does what is right! Their mouths are full of deceit, lies, and dangerous threats roll off their tongues as water (Romans 3:10-12)!

Not only is this true of them, but their speech is filled with unimaginable vile and vulgar language. They are quick to hurt and kill; ruin, destruction, misery and mayhem clutter their way wherever they go (Romans 3:12-16, GW)! It is no wonder God declares them as being without hope (Ephesians 2:12). Is there a more fearful and hopeless situation for any person to be in than that of being *spiritually dead*?

THE PRINCIPLE GOVERNING THE SPIRITUALLY DEAD

This leads naturally to the fourth truth about those who are *spiritually dead*; certain principles govern their existence. When a person dies, his soul lives on; it does not disintegrates, wander about in space or seek another way of returning to the physical realm.

This fact must be stressed time and time again, especially to those *spiritually dead* and unsaved; there is no hope beyond the grave! Perhaps Our Lord Jesus Christ gives the greatest illustration of this reality in the sixteenth chapter of the Gospel of Luke (vv. 19-31).

In that passage of Scripture, Jesus gives what most regard as a parable (though I believe it to be a factual account) about an unnamed rich man and a poor man named Lazarus. Both men died. The poor man went to a place called Abraham's bosom while the rich man went to a place simply called torment. While Lazarus rested in Abraham's bosom, the rich man suffered physically, mentally and emotionally in the place called torment. So intense was the rich man's pain that he cried to Abraham, ". . . have mercy on me, and send Lazarus, that he may dip the tip of his finger in water, and cool my tongue; for I am tormented in this flame (v.24)".

Note Abraham's response to the rich man request to send an emissary to tell his family and friends about the place called torment, "between us and you there is a vast gulf fixed: so that they which would pass from hence to you cannot; neither can they pass to us, that would come from thence" (v. 26). Lazarus' statement to the rich man makes this fact clear; there was no way for him to cross over to his realm of existence. Furthermore, there was no means, or the possibility (as seemingly implied) of leaving either place and returning to the living.

One additional teaching is seen in this passage from Luke; prior to Christ's death and resurrection, everyone that died went to a place called 'hell'. According to Old Testament Scripture, Hades, or Hell, was the only place suited for the souls of the dead, regardless of whether they were saved or unsaved. Passages from the books of Psalms, Isaiah and Job prove this point (cf. Psalms 9:17; Isaiah 14:9; 66:24; Job 10:21-22). Although those passages are ambiguous in their explanation of Hades, or Hell, Jesus reveals and clarifies its purpose and inhabitants to us in Luke 16:19-31.

From His account, we learned that Hades consisted of two sections, one for the saved and one for the unsaved. It should be pointed out that this is perhaps the clearest discussion in Scripture about what happened to the people who died prior to the resurrection.

These words of our Lord to the thief on the cross recorded in Luke 23:46, "Verily I say unto thee, Today shalt thou be with me in paradise", helps us further understand Hades. Notice the two promises Jesus made to the thief. First, he would be with him in paradise that same day. Second, he (Jesus Christ), would be in paradise with him.

By implication, these two promises help and support the fact stated by Jesus in the Luke passage in the following way. On the cross, Jesus Christ actually died! He did not just seem to die, as some teach; but his death was as real as the thieves beside him. Further evidence of this fact is his last words, "Father, into thy hands I commend my spirit". John Gill writes this about Jesus' words recorded in Luke 23:46, ". . . not the Holy Spirit, nor his divine nature, but his human soul". (John Gill, *John Gill's Exposition,* Luke 23:46)

Jesus' own words regarding his death, along with Gill's exposition of Luke 23:46 emphasize Jesus' humanity and suffering. It also highlights the truth of Jesus' dual nature; that he is both divine and human. Since He is God and cannot die, the only plausible explanation of his death is found in his humanity! This infinite fact about Jesus Christ being both God and man is one the finite mind can only wrestle with; and yet never began to comprehend.

This brings up the obvious question, "Would God send Jesus' spirit to a place of torment"? The answer to this perplexing question need not be drawn from speculation or theories because the book of the Psalms provides the answer, "For thou wilt not leave my soul to Sheol (Hell);

neither wilt thou suffer thy holy one to see corruption" (Psalms 16:10, my emphasis).

On the surface, it appears David is talking about himself in this Psalm. However, in the historical New Testament book of Acts, through divine inspiration, we learn that when David spoke of the 'holy one', he had in view Jesus Christ (Acts 2:27-29). We know this to be one of Jesus Christ's titles because the demonic forces used it during his earthy ministry (Mark 1:24; Luke 4:34).

With this being the case, it is irrational to imagine or believe that the 'Holy One of God' would descend to the place of torment, despite the teachings of some denominations today. Add to this, the fact, Jesus did not promise the other thief he would be with him. This alone proves that Jesus and the repentant thief were going to the section of Hell or Hades called 'paradise' or 'Abraham's bosom'.

Since Luke is the only Gospel that alludes to, and explains how this is possible, I believe it is safe to conclude that the place Jesus called Paradise is the same as Abraham's Bosom in Luke chapter sixteen. Other passages; such as the fourth chapter of Ephesians (4:9), and the third chapter of First Peter (3:19), support the teaching of Jesus' spirit going to a place of bliss and not suffering.

SPIRITUAL DEATH AND THE SIN NATURE

This section of the chapter is not designed to present a detailed discourse on the doctrine of Hell. Instead, its focus is to provide evidence to the fact that death does not mean the end of a person's existence. The soul (a person's *nature* and *personhood*) is the essence of every person. When a person dies, it has to go to a place suitable for its continued existence, a place governed by laws unlike those in the physical realm.

The second purpose of this section is to highlight the fact that death by its mere nature suggests separation. As stated earlier, every living person belongs to one of two realms. One consisting of those who are spiritually alive, or have a spiritual relationship to God, and the other consisting of those spiritually separated, or who have no relationship to God.

Citizens of both realms are recognized (although, not always) by their behavior, commitment, and loyalty to their master. The difference being, those who are spiritually alive, have the ability to willingly submit to their king or willingly disobey him. On the other hand, those *spiritually dead* have no such power. They are slaves in the truest sense of the word; unable to resist the will and power of their own nature and the overwhelming power of its rule over their whole being.

Man in his pride ridicules the idea of being a slave to his *nature*, but the Bible not only stress this fact, and does so strongly, it explains why. Take, for example, the seventh chapter of Paul's letter to the Christians at Rome, "For the good that I would I do not: but the evil which I would not, that I do. Now if I do that I would not, it is no more I that do it, but sin that dwelleth in me. I find then the law, that, to me who would do good, evil is present" (vs. 19-20).

Do you see man's struggle with his own *nature* in that verse? He wants to do good, but instead he does evil! Is it because he chooses to do so? According to the passage, it is only because of a greater *force* within him called *sin*, not the action, but the source producing the action, the *sin force* that now controls his *nature*, which in turn controls him! This brings us back to the discussion on *personhood*. The person that knows certain actions are wrong because the Bible says so, or was taught they are wrong, obviously does not want to do them. However, he or she cannot help but do them, no matter how hard they try to resist.

Romans 7:19-20 offers the only logical explanation as to why this is always the case. A real law is at work and like any law or principle; it is irresistible and unchangeable, unless overpowered by a greater force. For example, take the law of gravity. No clear thinking person would ever expect it not to work when applied; in other words, a dropped coin will always fall to the ground. This is the law of gravity! However, take that same coin to the Moon and drop it, and a different law makes it levitate. What changed? Not the coin but a different law at work which causes the coin to behave differently.

Though crude and simplistic, this example helps our understanding of this law spoken of by the Apostle Paul. It works within people unhindered. Add to this the fact mankind lives in a world dominated by the devil and his demonic forces, and you have a winless situation. As the prince of this world, the devil tempts people, saved and unsaved, with the riches and pleasures of this world through our sin nature (see image on next page).

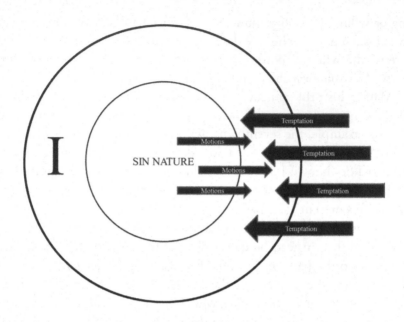

The Relationship Between Temptation and the Motions of sin

This is the state of man when born into this world, a slave to the *sin force* which rule through his own *nature*. Add to these two obstacles the fact, his world is under the power and influence of the devil. In his own power, man is unable to bring about any change to his situation. He believes he has the ability, but in reality, he is just as powerless to effect his situation, as the person who is dead physically.

However, there is hope for man! A way is provided to rescue him from himself and his *sin nature,* and set him free. But it is not possible without first being brought to realize his sad and permanent condition. And here is the problem, is it not? Born *spiritually dead,* trapped in a world of *sin* and under the power of Satan, how can he see his need? Add to these facts, man's utter hatred of God and his son Jesus Christ; who is the only person capable of saving him, and you have man's worse possible predicament.

However, all is not lost because before God determined in eternity to create the world and humanity, he saw Adam's fall and set in place a plan to redeem man from his sin! The only insight given to us by God regarding this wondrous plan is recorded by the Apostle Paul in these words, "According as he hath chosen us in him before the foundation of the world" (Ephesians 1:4a).

This grand and divine plan conceived and planned by God the Father, executed by God the Son and applied to those elected from mankind by God the Holy Spirit will be the subject of the upcoming chapters.

QUESTIONS TO PONDER

1. What is the significance of believing that Adam acted as humanity's Federal Head?
2. What other evidence could you present to the skeptic to show that all of humanity suffers because of the one act of disobedience by Adam?
3. How do you understand "made in the image of God"?
4. Discuss the relationship between personhood and the sin force.
5. What are some similarities between physical and spiritual death? How do they help us better understand the biblical definition of spiritual death?
6. How does the sixth chapter of Romans help you understand man's enslavement to his sin nature?

CHAPTER 5

Election and God's Plan of Salvation

The Bible declares God's *unconditional election* of a specific people before the foundation of the world to declare his glory throughout the earth(Ephesians 1:3, 5, 11). He did this, not because of any foreseen goodness in them, but solely because of his love!

Next to God sending his Son to die for us, *election* (the author's opinion) is the greatest manifestation of God's love (John 3:16). This statement is based on the fact that, without *election,* there would be no reason for God to send his Son into the world. As indicated in the last three chapters, man had no hope of ever saving himself. Everything was against him: the sin force, his own corrupt nature, his depraved condition, his severed relationship with God, his inclination towards sin and ultimately the devil himself. As the Apostle Paul states in his letter to the church at Ephesus, man was "without God in the world" (Ephesians 2:11). Add to these facts; man is hostile and enemies of God (Romans 5:8, 10), spiritually dead (Ephesians 2:5), and sinners eternally condemned (Romans 1:18), and you have the complete picture of utter hopelessness and despair.

To speak of such beings as possessing the ability to recognize their need for a savior, let alone their wretched state, is inconceivable. Only man in his arrogance and pride, believes such an action on his part is possible. Again, the reality of it all, and here is the glory of *election,* if God had not elected from a humanity that was doomed and destined for hell and ultimately the lake of fire, nobody would be saved!

Perhaps the idea of God's grace and mercy was in the mind of the 18th century slave trader, John Newton when he penned the words comprising the first stanza of the well-known hymn, *Amazing Grace,*

> Amazing Grace, How sweet the sound,
> That saved a wretch like me

I once was lost, but now I'm found
Was blind, but now I see

Do you see in Newton's mind the marvel and awe of God's grace? How else could any person ever hope to escape the flames of Hell if not by God's election? Lost sinners; wretched, blind, evil, and dead to the things of God (Ephesians 2:12; Romans. 5:6); Ephesians 2:1, 12), that is the description of all humankind when born into this world! Wrestle with the reality of those negatives as John Newton did and the thought alone is enough to drive one to the precipice of despair! Only God, with arms outstretched could drag us away from that precipice and into His loving arms; which he did through his devine plan of *election*!

WHAT IS ELECTION

Election comes from a Greek word meaning to select or choose something based on the willing choice of another. A classic illustration of *election* is the consumer going to the market and selecting apples or some other produce from a basket or other type container. Why does the person choose one over the others? Is it not based on their own choice and desires? This is a tangible analogy of *election*.

But let us look at the biblical explanation and example of this doctrine given in the ninth chapter of the book of Romans. There, Paul gives an illustration of a potter who, from a common lump of clay, chooses to make vessels according to his desires. Paul raises the question, "Hath not the potter power over the clay, of the same lump to make one vessel unto honor, and another unto dishonor" (Romans 9:21)?

His argument is straightforward and takes us back to the earlier example of the consumer; both were faced with a choice. The consumer chose the products he, or she liked, just as the potter can make from the same clay a beautiful vase or an ordinary flower pot. It's their choice! A closer examination of the potter reveals another fundamental truth about *election*; he makes the vessels from one lump of clay.

This is analogous to the existing condition of humanity as a whole. In a sense, all of us are essentially part of one lump, or mass of beings that originated from one person—Adam! Barring race, creed, nationality and ethnicity, there is nothing about any single person that distinguished or separate us one from another spiritually. All were guilty (Psalms 53, Romans 3:23)! All were condemned since all were sinners!

The Guilt of All Humanity

But God, who is rich in mercy and grace, looked beyond time, beyond creation and Adam's disobedience and selected from that one lump, some to salvation while passing over the others, leaving them in their sinful condition.

To bring out the glory of God's grace and mercy, J. Dwight Pentecost writes, "God is a God whose disposition is such towards a sinner that, spontaneously, mercy flows out from Him to meet mankind's miseries". (Pentecost, *Sound Doctrine*, 20) In essence, the doctrine of *election* demonstrates God's favorable disposition towards the lump of lost humanity who deserves the wrath and eternal punishment of God, the potter!

ELECTION: A MANIFESTATION OF GOD'S SOVEREIGNTY

But note an additional fact about the potter; the lump of clay belonged to him. Perhaps he purchased the clay or secured it by his own hands in some other way. In either case, it belonged to him! He owned it! In a much stronger sense, all of humanity belongs to God, atheist and agnostic alike, because he created us. Therefore, both saved,and unsaved are his, the only difference between the two is found in their relationship to him. So when God chose some to be saved while passing over others, he is entirely justified in his actions. None can complain or boast because the action from start to finish was based on his plan and choice (Philippians 1:6)!

Paul helps our understanding of this aspect of *election* when he asks the question, "O man, who art thou that repliest against God? Shall the thing formed say to him that formed it, Why hast thou made me so" (Romans 9:20)? Paul based this argument on the perceived objection of those passed over by God.

This is the significance of using an inanimate object to illustrate humanity's plight. As people who are born into the physical world spiritually dead, we lay helpless in the graveyard of sin. In this state, we are as lifeless and passive spiritually just as much as the lump of clay. We lack the ability to remove ourselves from this grave or call out for help.

The clay is entirely dependent upon the potter, to buy it, bring it to his shop, pick it up, mold it, and shape it; in order to become the object desired by the potter. All this is based solely on the potter's right. The clay in Paul's illustration is a representation and portrayal of fallen humanity after Adam's disobedience, one wholly dependent on God's grace.

ELECTION: A MANIFESTATION OF GOD'S GRACE

Is God's action in choosing some to be saved while rejecting others just (Romans 9:17)? From a human standpoint, it does not seem so. But here again, God is not judged by human thinking, but his own wisdom. According to Scripture, God's answer to man's objection is this, "What if God, willing to show his wrath, and to make his power known, endured with much longsuffering the vessels of wrath fitted to destruction" (Romans 9:22).

Note the beginning of this verse, 'What if God'. The first observation about this portion of the verse is the word 'What'. In the original writing, Paul omitted this word and started the verse this way, "If God willing . . ." Dr. Lloyd-Jones comments that, Paul, "starts with a condition . . . but he never gives us the conclusion". (Lloyd-Jones, D. M. *Romans: An Exposition of Chapter 9, God's Sovereign Purpose*. Edinburgh, Scotland: The Banner of Truth Trust,1991, 210)

To understand the meaning of Romans 9:22, the reader must remember that this verse is part of the larger context that started in Romans 9:19. Paul's thought is still on the potter and his right to take what is his (the lump) and make it into whatever he choose. With that thought in mind, Paul now declares, "What objection can there be to that"? (Lloyd-Jones,

Romans, An Exposition of Chapter 9, 210) That's the significance behind Paul beginning the verse as he did.

The next word, 'willing', further highlight God's right to do as he please with humanity. The Greek word used in this verse means to, 'be strongly inclined to do something'. Jamieson, Fausset and Brown translate the phrase, 'willing to show', in Romans 9:22, as, "designing to manifest". (*JFB*, Romans 9:22-23) Their explanation regarding the term willing highlights two aspects of God's character. First: is God's holiness as it relates to sin. Keep in mind, the focus is still on the reasoning behind God's election of some from fallen humanity while passing over others.

With that thought in mind, it becomes apparent that if God saved all of humanity, it proves that the world's concept of God is true after all; that he is all loving, all forgiving, and overlooks evil and does not punish sin. The Bible knows nothing of this God. Instead, its characterization is clear; God abhors sin in any form because he is holy! That was the main reason the first chapter of this book focused on God's holiness. It is his holiness that inclines, and inclines him strongly to punish sin!

However, extreme caution must be exercised when making such strong statements regarding God's treatment of sin in order to avoid portraying God as being capricious; who inflicts his wrath upon people just because he can. To the contrary, Scripture declares this about God's attitude towards the wicked, "As I live, saith the Lord GOD, I have no pleasure in the death of the wicked" (Ezekiel 33:11). I suppose, if God was capricious in his actions towards humanity, it would certainly have perished millennia ago. No, the Bible makes clear that his desire is, "that the wicked turn from his way and live".

Therefore, the problem is not with God, but man's natural tendency to commit sin and God's hatred of it. This hatred of sin is displayed in his wrath upon those he did not choose to salvation, and those referred to by Paul as "vessels fitted for destruction".

If you notice, in Romans 9:20 and 21, a lump of clay was Paul's emphasis. However, in Romans 9:22, Paul change his focus and draws the reader's attention to the term vessels. Dr. Lloyd-Jones explains that Paul's change of focus from clay to vessels is intended to highlight the fact that the lump (v. 21), was more of a general characterization of humanity as a whole, while vessels particularizes it as consisting of individual person (cf. Romans 1:18; Luke 3:7; 21:23; 2 Thessalonians 2:9). In doing so, the Spirit highlights the fact that every single human being (symbolized by vessel) is guilty and worthy of God's wrath. This is the thinking behind the term 'fitted'. (Lloyd-Jones, *Romans, An Exposition of Chapter 9*, 213)

However, even though these facts accurately describe sinful humanity, God does not restrain his goodness. He still allows the sun to shine on all in equal abundance. The rain provides nourishment to the earth, so food is available to sustain both animals and humans. God gives us strength and resources to work and provide for our families.

These and many more graces the LORD God sends; not simply to some, but both good and evil, rich and poor, and the *elect* and non-elect. In other words, 'He endured with much longsuffering the vessels of wrath fitted to destruction'.

ELECTION: A MANIFESTATION OF GOD'S GLORY

But notice secondly, not only do we see God's holiness and hatred of sin, we also see in Romans 9:23 "the riches of his glory". Attempts to explain the attributes and nature of God is not only difficult, it is overwhelming to the finite mind. It actually comes down to the question, "How does the finite mind describe the infinite"? Like trying to explain to a small child the Laws of physics, our minds cannot even begin to comprehend the greatness of God's existence, and even with the help of the Holy Spirit, our words are still inadequate.

This is especially true when it comes to God's glory; or essentially who he is. There are instances in the New Testament where the Apostle Paul and other do the best they can in describing God's glory. Take for example, Paul's closing comments in the eleventh chapter of Romans, "O the depth of the riches both of the wisdom and knowledge of God! How unsearchable are his judgments, and his ways past finding out" (Romans 11:33)!

Do you see his struggle? He can't seem to find the right Adjectives to describe God and the wisdom demonstrated in saving us! It's too deep, too high, too wide and too broad; it's impossible to find out! That's not only his problem, but all those who have been given a glimpse or taste of God's wondrous wisdom and glory. So it's not surprising that he uses this phrase when making the second factual statement regarding God's election; it manifests the riches of his glory!

The imagery is clear, is it not? Riches conjure up in one's thoughts and reasoning, an unlimited resource. It has no end, no boundaries and no restrictions. In defining God's glory and its use in Romans 9:23, "His glorious riches", has reference to "the perfections of his nature, his love, grace, and mercy, his wisdom, power, faithfulness, justice, and holiness; all which are most evidently displayed in the salvation of his people". (*JFB*, Romans 9:22-23)

Surely this is what the Spirit was conveying through Paul when he penned those words. Whatever God does, he does infinitely and gloriously because that's who he is. So when the finite mind see his works through physical eyes, it stands in awe and reverence, it marvels at the fact that such a powerful and infinite God would take the time to *elect* "vessels fitted for destruction" and make known the riches of his glory 'on the vessels of mercy'.

Notice the way the word *vessels* is used in Romans 9:22 and 23. First, in verse 22, it is "vessels fitted for destruction". These vessels represent people who were not chosen by God for salvation. They are left under God's wrath, judgment and condemnation. Remember, the focus is on God's willingness (defined as God's inclination) to show his wrath and power in punishing sinful humanity for its sin. He could have chosen to bestow his grace and mercy on these vessels, but he did not.

But in verse 23, which is a continuation of verse 22, we see something else that God is inclined to do, something else he is willing to do, not upon the vessels mentioned in verse 22, but a different group. On them, he shows, not his wrath, but his mercy! The key in verse 23 is the little word, 'on'. These people are not unique, they have done nothing to earn, or deserve God's favor; yet He shows them mercy by holding back deserved punishment. (Lloyd-Jones, *Romans, An Exposition of Chapter 9*, 224)

Remember, these are from the same lump, the same mass of condemned humanity. They all belong to God, who, has the authority and ability, to do as he please with each one of them. They all were essentially 'fitted for destruction' initially, but because of the 'riches of his glory', some were set aside; or chosen for his glory. This is what's behind *election;* God's willingness to show his wrath and ability to deal with sin; and to show the riches of his glory by showing mercy towards those whom he *elected.*

This is why the famous Reformer, Martin Luther's singled out the doctrine of *election* as the 'Core Ecclesia', that is, the 'core of the Church'. Implied in Luther's statement is this fact: *election* is the core of all other Christian doctrine. Put bluntly, to reject or de-emphasize it is to miss the grandeur and immensity of God's sovereignty, love, grace and 'the riches of his glory'!

ELECTION: SOLELY OF GOD

When most Christians are pressed about the role of *election* in salvation, the most common answer given is of God looking down the portals of time, and *electing* individuals based on their decision to choose him. This exalted view underscores man's ignorance regarding the scope of the sin force and its total control over every aspect of our being. As stated in the previous chapters, people sin, not because they want to, but because the sin nature compels them through their nature.

Therefore, it goes without saying that since man lacks the ability to save himself, he needs the power of another to, not only help him, but rescue him from his hopeless and miserable condition. However, in order for this to happen, a person must first realize they're in trouble, and there lies the problem. How can a person who is spiritually dead, not so much realize their predicament, but gather up the desire and strength to leave it?

They cannot do so on their own because the sin force, working through their nature and members, blinds their hearts and mind (cf. Ephesians 2:2-3; 4:18)! Though they hear the message of salvation with their physical ears through all sorts of channels, they cannot respond. It's like the impotent beggar, who sits within arms-length of a coin, but cannot reach out to take it because his arms and legs lack the power to do so.

Though radical and extreme, this example, though far from perfect, portrays, not some, but all of humanity prior to salvation! A picture of men and women having hands, but cannot use them to reach out to the Savior; of men and women having feet, yet unable to run from God's wrath to his loving arms, and men and women with tongues, yet unable to respond to God's call! No wonder the question was asked by the disciples; how is it possible for anyone to be saved (Mark 10:26)? The answer rests in all that's been said from the previous section of this chapter; God must act upon these 'vessels fitted for destruction'.

I almost hesitate to say this, but I side with Luther, Calvin, and Augustine regarding the importance of this particular doctrine of our faith. As a matter of fact, I agree with Luther that *election* is the, 'Core of the Church'. No other doctrine of our faith so clearly defend and set forth

God's sovereignty; and ultimately his immense love, for those who would never love him, if left to their own volition.

I also strongly believe, that despite the strong opposition against it, there are few other doctrines of our faith whose reality is presented in so many illustrations and evidences in Scripture as is *election*! Following are a few examples.

ELECTION ILLUSTRATED: ABRAHAM'S CALL

The first picture of *election* is the Patriarch Abraham. A cursory examination of his life reveals a man, though rich by today's standard, was still just an ordinary man, who knew nothing of the Christian God or his laws. Like everyone in his country of Ur, monotheism was the furthest thing from his thoughts or behavior. (Unger, Merrill F. *Unger Bible Dictionary, Third Ed.* Chicago, Illinois: Moody Press, 1966, 1127) Based on his life and worship, do you see one worthy of the title, 'father of the faithful' or 'friend of God'? Yet Scripture makes both declarative statements about him. The question becomes, "How did Abraham rise to such prominence"?

To be fair, I might add that the famous Jewish historian Flavius Josephus paints a somewhat different view of Abraham's early days in Ur. In his Antiquities of the Jews, he gives this account, "He was the first that ventured to publish this notion, that there was but one God, the creator of the universe; and that, as to other [gods] if they contributed anything to the happiness of men, that each of them afforded it only according to his appointment, and not by their own country". (*Josephus, Antiquities of the Jews*, II.VII.1)

I am certainly in no position to judge or contradict this acclaimed historian. But since Abraham lived more than 3000 years before Josephus, I believe the biblical account of Abraham's life is more reliable. This is not to say there were no writings from that period, nor can it be said those writings were inaccurate. But like any historian, Josephus wrote from his own view of history and therefore, his portrayal of the father of his nation is going to be as favorable as possible. Besides, he betrays his belief in the possibility of gods other than the one God in his statement, "and that, as to other [gods] if they contributed anything to the happiness of men". The Bible, on the other hand, portrays Abraham as an ordinary man flawed by doubts, unfaithfulness, anxiety and other inhibitions attributable to all men.

Yet despite his shortcomings, the Bible still tells us that God called him and only him, out from among his countrymen. Hear God's words to Abram (Abraham), "Get thee out of thy country, and from thy kindred, and from thy father's house, unto a land that I will shew thee". (Genesis 12:2) This verse is commonly referred to as God's call to Abraham. Here, we get another relevant word relating to election: *called*. It literally means to *summon* in both the Old and New Testament. The picture is of one who is *summoned* out from among a group or class of people by another.

Is there a better explanation of what happened to Abraham, who lived in Ur of the Chaldeans, where the moon god Nannar and his wife Ningal were essential objects of worship. (Unger, *Unger Bible Dictionary,* 1127) Furthermore, Josephus record that Noah had five sons, "who inhabited the land that began at Euphrates, and reached to the Indian Ocean". Of these five sons, Josephus records that, "Arphaxad named the Arphaxadites, who are now called Chaldeans". (*Josephus, Antiquities of the Jews,* II.VI.4)

As pictured on the map of the Ancient Near East at the bottom of this page; the area settled by Arphaxad and his descendants was located in the lower portion of the Fertile Crescent in a country known as Ur.

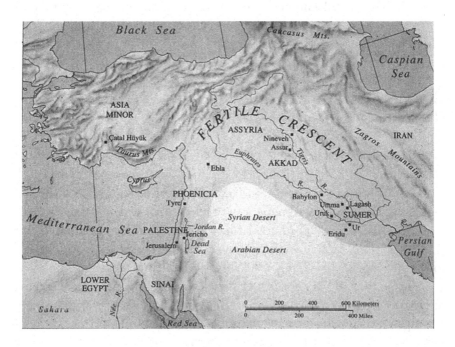

Map of the Ancient Near East

To further support Josephus' facts, the Bible includes Arphaxad in Abraham's lineage, in both the book of Genesis (10:24) and the third chapter of the Gospel of Luke (v. 36). Another note of interest regarding Arphaxad, his grandson's (from his first son Salah or Sala)), name was Heber from which, according to Josephus, is where the name Hebrew comes. (*Josephus, Antiquities of the Jews*, II.VI.4)

One might ask, "Why rely on this historical data from Josephus and not his portrayal of Abraham". The answer is simple. These are historical accounts of the Jewish nation. Their trustworthiness is based on the Jews' known zeal for maintaining the accurate portrayal of their history. And besides, both secular and religious history provides an accurate picture of the Chaldean religious practices. Their brutality and idol worship leaves little room to believe they ever believed in or worshipped the one true God.

This was the setting in which Abraham lived, and the one from which God *called* him. While one can speculate, as Berosus did in his assertion that Abraham might have been the only 'righteous and great' man living among the Chaldeans, Scripture declares, "There is none righteous, no not one" (Romans 3:10)! This declaration is not limited to the first century, or during David or Abraham's day; but finds its origin in the Garden of Eden when Adam ate from the tree of the knowledge of good and evil. From that point in human history, the essence of man's nature was evil!

ELECTION ILLUSTRATED: ABRAHAM'S EMPOWERMENT TO RESPOND TO GOD'S CALL

The first fact we learn about God's *calling* is that God *summons* and the person being summoned is entirely passive. The subject does not seek God's *call* (Romans 3:11) and, in fact, is not even aware of it until God makes that *call* known. Abraham responded to God's *call* solely because God gave him the ability to do so. This is the second extraordinary truth about God's *call*; he enables or empowers the individual *called*, to respond to his *call*. He literally changes the person's disposition towards him!

This is perhaps the greatest evidence that Abraham was not serving or worshipping the one true God. His constitution was not conducive to serving or hearing his voice, let alone obeying him. While it's true, he could possibly recognize that there was a greater god than those worshipped by his countrymen; but he did not have the mental capacity to persuade or help him understand the God of creation. As discussed in chapter two, he had grasped the reality of God from the facts presented to him through general revelation, but it could take him no further. It could not help him realize his need for God, nor could it help him engage personally with this God of creation, who reveals himself through his word and Spirit.

Paul helps us understand Abraham's dilemma when it comes to understanding God's Word (and every one prior to being saved), in the first chapter of his letter to the Christians in Rome. Notice what he says, "For the wrath of God is revealed from heaven against all ungodliness and unrighteousness of men, who hold the truth in unrighteousness" (Romans 1:18).

The key word in this passage is 'hold'. This word is generally understood in a positive sense when spoken in our language, but in this passage, it is used to emphasize people's natural hostility towards God and his truth. Paul wants us to see that although the truth of God is clearly laid out plain for everyone to see, people actually suppress those truths and refuse to allow their mind to process them. Not because they do not want to, but because the sin force at work in their nature will not let them! Like Abraham, Moses or David, or any of the other thousands of godly men and women of all ages, unless God acts upon our evil nature and override the sin force at work within us, we cannot know Him. If we cannot know Him, how can we expect to love, seek, believe, and finally respond to His *call*?

This is man's plight, establishing a personal relationship with—not a god—but God! How can he take what has been revealed naturally and transition it over into the realm of spiritual understanding. These are strong statements, and they must be stated in this way simply because what's in view is spiritual understanding, and not man's natural ability to arrive at a rationale conclusion on his own!

So when we think of Abraham or anyone else, and their response to God, all these facts must be considered; the sin force in us and people's natural desire to suppress God's truth about his state. I must stress that the previous negative statements made about Abraham and his relationship to God were by no means an indictment against him. Instead, they were given to explain the fact, that apart from the power of God acting on and in us, it is impossible for any person to know him.

This is the only reason Abraham was able to respond to God; or to put it another way, God supernaturally changed Abraham's disposition, enabling him to hear and respond to His voice. In essence, Abraham received a new birth that took him from spiritual death to spiritual life, from darkness to life and into a new relationship with God. Whereas, before he was ignorant to the things of God, now he loved them!

Election Illustrated: The Nation Of Israel

Abraham is not the only picture of God's plan through *election*. Another and perhaps more compelling one is the nation of Israel. It's difficult to see God's *election* of persons, especially most of the ones recorded in Scripture, even Abraham. But when it comes to Israel, that difficulty is somewhat lessened if not removed entirely, not so much by her preservation, but her restoration as a nation.

No other nation in the annals of history, can boast of their destruction, and its inhabitants, not just scattered, but lost in the valley of the nations (Ezekial 37:1). Her identity as a nation; both in name and identity, ceased after the fall of Jerusalem in A.D. 70. The immensity of Israel's destruction was such that the prophet Ezekiel characterized the entire nation as being dead (Ezekiel 37).

Yet this same nation was reborn and recognized by the United Nation as a sovereign nation in 1948. Despite her relatively small size, and against overwhelming odds at times, she continues to exist in the midst of hostility, with minimum assistance from outside sources. Her armed forces are recognized as being among the best in the world and showed during the six-day war of 1967. And even in that war, she was preserved by God's mighty power and not her own (cf. Daniel 12:1).

How has she been able to survive since her inception? Is it because of her own power, or desire to survive? To the natural eye this might appear to be the case. However, the biblical student understands that there is a much grandeur plan at work regarding Israel, because her survival is based, not on their ability or military power; but God's love for her and his promise to Abraham. Hear God's words to Israel in her infancy, "Jehovah did not set his love upon you, nor choose you, because ye were more in number than any people; for ye were the fewest of all people: but because Jehovah loveth you, and because he would keep the oath which he sware unto your fathers, hath Jehovah brought you out with a mighty hand, and redeemed you out of the house of bondage, from the hand of Pharaoh king of Egypt" (Deuteronomy 7:7, 8).

Is there any room for boasting in that passage? None at all! For example, what reason did God gives for *selecting* Israel over the Egyptians? Certainly not because of their might, because she had none! Nor were they *chosen* because of their technological advances in architecture, warfare or marvellous institutes of learning. None of these things characterized the Hebrew people, yet Jehovah chose them for these two reasons: 1) He loved them, and 2) His promise to Abraham, Isaac and Jacob.

All this; the choice of Abraham, the choice of Isaac over Ishmael, Jacob over Esau and finally Israel over all the nations of the world, were all of God! These are hardly the wishful thinking of Judaism and later fostered by Christianity, since secular historians, Jewish, as well as others, confirm the facts presented in the Holy Bible regarding the nation of Israel. In doing so, they unknowingly confirms God's plan which is simply this: through the one man Abraham he would bring the one nation called Israel who would give birth to the One and only Savior, Jesus Christ! The famous song writer, Augustus Toplady, summed this up in these words,

> Could my tears forever flow, Could my zeal no languor know
> These for sin could not atone; Thou must save, and Thou alone;
> In my hand no price I bring; simply to thy Cross I cling

QUESTIONS TO PONDER

1. What is election and why do you think Luther consider it as the "core of the Church"?
2. Why do you think the biblical definition and presentation of election is so difficult to accept, even among many Christians?
3. How has this chapter changed or helped your understanding of this doctrine?
4. How does election better help your understanding of God's love for the sinner?
5. Is election fair? Explain.

CHAPTER 6

Humanity's Inability to Come to Jesus

Election is not based on merit, deeds or goodness! As discussed in the previous chapter, Abraham and Israel are prime examples of this truth. Both were chosen by God just because it pleased him to do so. He did not look down the portals of time and see a man named Abraham choosing him when the opportunity presented itself. As stated earlier, while such thinking is the norm when it comes to *election*, there is nothing further from the truth, since it subjects a supreme and sovereign God to the whims of humanity. In a sense, it places God on the same level as his creation and relegates him to a position where he must constantly readjust his plans according to our will. Now ask yourself the question; is this Jehovah, the self-existent one, or the one who spoke the worlds into existence? Can this be the God of Sinai or the God who parted the Red Sea?

Unfortunately, many Christians see no contradiction between God's sovereignty and peoples' freedom of choice. They gladly assert man's autonomy over God's sovereignty. To them, this represents a perfect balance between God's will and man's freedom. To be fair, I believe many who maintain and teach this concept do so with the belief they are somehow upholding and guarding God's character.

While such thinking is admirable, it actually does just the opposite because the one fact made throughout the Bible is this: God is the supreme sovereign! Arthur Pink writes this about God as the supreme sovereign, "The supremacy of the true and living God might well be argued from the infinite distance which separates the mightiest creatures from the almighty Creator. He is the Potter, they are but the clay in His hands to be molded into vessels of honor, or to be dashed into pieces (Psalm 2-9) as He pleases". (Pink, *Attributes*, 31)

Pink further writes, "Were all the denizens of heaven and all the inhabitants of the earth to combine in revolt against Him, it would occasion Him no uneasiness, and would have less effect upon His eternal and unassailable Throne than has the spray of Mediterranean's waves upon the towering rocks of Gibraltar. So puerile and powerless is the creature to affect the Most High, Scripture itself tells us that when the Gentile heads unite with apostate Israel to defy Jehovah and His Christ, "He that sitteth in the heavens shall laugh". (Pink, *Attributes*, 31) This is the character of the God of Scripture; once people fully accept this truth, such doctrines as election, predestination and God's decree will be embraced without reservation. I also believe that a proper understanding of election gives the Christian a better insight and a greater awareness of God's love, grace, and mercy.

What is the Biblical Teaching On Election?

Other than what has already been discussed in the previous chapter, what else does the Bible teach about *election*? This question must be asked because too many Christians believe that God's choice in election is based primarily, if not solely, on the fact that he saw them exercising faith in his Son at some point in time. Such teaching if viewed through spectacles after Adam's sin would see how ridiculous the whole thing is. A person comes to Jesus, not because of a natural desire, but because God empowers them to come!

Before proceeding, I want to emphasize that the facts presented in this section regarding *election* are based on scriptural teachings from the Holy Bible. However, having said that, the author realize that not all (whether Christian or non-Christian) will agree on the specifics of *election* as I will present them. Since the focus is not to change one's thinking about this critical teaching, but instead allow the Holy Spirit to illumine the reader's mind as only he can, comments will be limited to extracting from the text, as best as possible, what I believe it actually says. The safest way of doing this is to rely on the original language and the context of each passage used.

As stated earlier, the purpose of the last chapter was to help the reader understand; God has a plan for saving a select group of people. Additionally, the chapter stressed that this plan is illustrated in His *selection* of Abraham and the nation Israel.

This chapter continues that discussion by bringing in some of the specifics of the doctrine of *election*. But, before we begin our discussion, we need to address this question: "Where in the Bible is this teaching found, if at all"? The most common answer given is Romans 8:28 and Ephesians 1:4.

It goes without saying that these two passages are best known and most quoted when *election* is taught, and rightly so. However, they are not the first place in the New Testament where this teaching is mentioned. Instead, it comes from the lips of our Lord in the sixth chapter of John's Gospel in these words, "No man can come to me, except the Father which hath sent me draw him" (John 6:44a).

Let's briefly examine this verse. The first thing is Jesus' declaration that 'no man' is able to come to him apart from the Father's drawing. Some might say, "The phrase 'no man' has reference only to the Jews or his immediate audience. However, the context clearly indicates his response is based on the crowd's opposition to his claims of coming from heaven in verse thirty-eight and being the bread of life in verse thirty-five. While the immediate audience was Jewish, his response should not be seen as being exclusive to them. This is not an assumption on my part but is drawn from Jesus' earlier statement given in verse thirty-three that he is the bread given from God, not only to or for Jews; but the world.

That being the context of the passage, the only conclusion one could draw regarding the identity of those identified by the phrase 'no man' is that Jesus must have had in view the same group identified as 'the world' in verse thirty-three. This is simple Hermeneutics (science of interpreting the Bible) and should present little dispute or disagreement. Therefore, Jesus' declarative statement in this verse is that no man can come to him, except something happens first. Regarding this verse, Dr. R. C. Sproul stress that the word, ". . . can has to do with ability, not permission".[1]

After reading Dr. Sproul's comment, I wanted to know why he felt it necessary to place special emphasis on the meaning of this particular word. So I went to the *Free Dictionary by Farlex* for clarity. Here is how it defines *can*: "Used to indicate physical or mental ability". In its Usage Notes for this word, *Farlex* adds, "Generations of grammarians and teachers have insisted that can should be used only to express the capacity to do something, and that 'may' must be used to express permission".

---

1   Taken from *CHOSEN BY GOD* by R.C. Sproul. Copyright © 1986 by R.C. Sproul. Used by permission of Tyndale House Publishers, Inc. All rights reserved.

This statement along with the definition from *Farlex* not only helped my understanding of Dr. Sproul's teaching, but also the reason why Jesus chose this particular word in John 6:44. I believe he did not want to be ambiguous about this area of salvation. In doing so, he removed all doubts and questions about man's inability to come to him. This is a comprehensive and declarative statement comparative to his response to Nicodemus regarding the new birth, "Ye must be born again" (John 3:7).

Another reason Jesus' statement should be interpreted universally is seen in his use of the phrase no man. This is an extremely strong phrase that comes from a compound Greek word meaning, 'not one' or 'not even one'.

Do you see the relationship between man's ability and his inability when it comes to, coming to Jesus? No one, that is, not even one person has the capacity to come to Jesus by his or her own power or will. This is perhaps the strongest defense for election because the phrase used by Jesus leaves no one out. Again, not to be redundant, but this fact further highlight the reality of man's spiritual death and the principles governing it, even their ability to choose Christ as their Savior!

LOGICAL OPPOSITION TO ELECTION

This teaching goes against the prevailing thought process of most Christians. One reason is a misunderstanding of the twelfth verse of the first chapter of the Gospel of John, which states, "But as many as received him, to them gave he power to become the sons of God, even to them that believe on his name". Again, on the surface, and if taken by itself, it seems to imply the choice of coming to Jesus lies within one's own ability. However, any verse (even this one), when taken in isolation can support any teaching, especially one that is used out of context.

For the sake of argument, let's assume John 1:12 was the only passage of Scripture available regarding our salvation. Does it support the idea of anyone being able to come to Jesus on their own? Again, on the surface, the verse does seem to support this truth, that is, until we come to the end of the verse where we read, "even to them that believe on his name".

Right away, a requirement is set forth; one must first believe on Jesus' name, and how does that happen? According to the tenth chapter of Romans, it comes first by hearing the Gospel message and then by exercising faith (Romans 10:9-15). Do you see how difficult it is to take one verse and build an entire doctrine? The word believe forces us to go elsewhere in the Bible for clarification and a clearer understanding.

But even if we stayed with the initial assumption of John 1:12 as being the sole verse in the Bible regarding our salvation, it would still support Jesus' statement in John 6:44 from a grammatical standpoint in this way. In the American Standard and King James versions of the Bible, John 1:12 ends with a colon. One reason for using colons is to emphasize a point you want the reader to pay attention to. In the case of John 1:12, John makes a general statement about salvation. By putting a colon (and not a comma or semicolon as some translations does), the translators alerts or directs the reader's attention to the next verse. In essence, John was saying, my statement in verse 12 is incomplete! So to isolate the two verses is to present the half-truth that all a person has to do is believe on Jesus, and they will be saved.

While it is true that the verse does say that; a person should not go away from it, without knowing why it's true. That's the importance of reading verse thirteen, which provides the explanation or requirement, notice what it says, "Who were born, not of blood, nor of the will of the flesh, nor of the will of man, but of God". (John 1:13, ASV). In this verse, the Apostle John makes it clear that no one comes to Jesus, or is saved by, 'the will of the flesh'. We are saved by the will of God; he *chooses* whom to save. If he choose not to exercise his will in this way, a person simply cannot be saved! So you see, even if you just took this one passage, you're immediately taken back to the fundamental principle set forth by Jesus in the sixth chapter of John: "No man can come to me, except the Father that sent me draw him" (John 6:44, ASV).

The second principle seen in John 6:44 is the fact that a person comes to Jesus Christ because God *draws* them. Here is another fascinating term used by Jesus, it is a Greek word meaning to *drag*. To avoid putting forward a negative image of God, it is best to look at the twenty-first chapter of John where this same word is used. In verse six, we read, "They cast therefore, and now they were not able to draw it for the multitude of fishes" (John 21:6, ASV).

This verse gives us an accurate picture of what's going on in God's drawing. When catching fish, the fisherman has to cast his net into the sea. In doing so, he's able to catch fish of all different types. As a matter of fact, his catch is limited only by the capacity of his net. Once his net has been filled, he drags the fishes caught to shore or into the boat.

In other words, if the fishes are to be brought in, they must be dragged in by the fishermen. Note this interesting thing about the caught fish. They did not exercise their will to jump into the net, they were caught by the fishermen, not the other way around. That's the idea behind the term *drag*. If men and women, boys and girls from every walk of life are to come to Jesus, God must first catch them and *drag* them to his beloved son!

The greatest image of God's grace is seen here because he was and is under no obligation to draw or exercise His will favorably towards sworn enemies (Romans 5:10). Yet he does, and does so graciously. This is the essence of *election* and God's grace.

Before concluding this chapter, it is essential to emphasize that God does not *draw* capriciously nor does he *draw* by force. Instead, out of his matchless love, he so moves on the hearts and minds of the elect to the point that they willingly surrender their will to his, and come to him. In his commentary on this word, John Gill writes, "Drawing, though it supposes power and influence, yet not always coaction and force: music draws the ear, love the heart, and pleasure the mind". (John Gill, *John Gill's Exposition,* John 6:44) This is what's in view behind the word *drag*, God's loving and compassionate arms *calling* and *drawing* those whom he loves to himself and his Son through the power of the Holy Spirit.

QUESTIONS TO PONDER

1. Why does an improper understanding of election leads to a misunderstanding of how we're saved?
2. If a person does not believe in the doctrine of election, can they be saved?
3. Why would this doctrine not normally be discussed when talking to a non-Christian about salvation, i.e. as an element of evangelism?
4. Having read this chapter, how has it affected your thinking about election? About God's fairness? About God's grace

CHAPTER 7

The Foreknowledge and Omniscience of God

How great God's love must be for us! The most well known verse in the Bible is John 3:16, but have you ever actually thought about its meaning? Most everyone knows what it is to love someone, but our greatest expression of love is incomparable to God's, because he is the very essence of love (I John 4:16)!

Though ineffable and incomprehensible, men have attempted to communicate God's love in song, take for example, these words from Lehman's famous hymn,

> The love of God is greater far Than tongues or pen can ever tell;
> It goes beyond the highest star, and reaches to the lowest hell;

Can you not see the penman's mental frailty; not intellectually, but his own inadequacy as he attempts to explain something infinite! We empathize with him while at the same time yearning along with him to understand and know why God loves us so. Though we may spend a life time in this quest, at our dying breath we also will echo Lehman's words,

> O love of God, how rich and pure! How measureless and strong!
> It shall forever more endure, The saints and angels song.

This is the God of Scripture and the God of all Christians, the God who set his love upon us before the foundation of the world according to Scripture. How did he do this? The answer is given in the eighth chapter of Paul's letter to the Christians at Rome in these words, 'For whom he foreknew, he also foreordained'. The key word in this phrase, and I guess I should say the two key words since the one *(foreknew)* is no good *without foreordained.*

A MATTER OF CLARITY

Romans 8:28 is another well-known verse in the Bible. We all have either quoted it; posted it on our wall, placed it on our desk or some other conspicuous place in our home or office. And why not, it's one of the most magnificent and comforting promises of God. But a full appreciation of it is not grasp until we fully understand the nature of its truths. Take, for example, this first term, *foreknew.* Here, is a word one would expect to top the list of words in God's plan because it seems to speak of God's *omniscience.*

However, God's *omniscience* is not the focus of this particular word, at least not directly. Are you amazed and awe struck by the wisdom of God? Because he is infinite in knowledge and understanding, the obvious question becomes; how does such a being communicate with finite creatures?

In the Old Testament, God chose to reveal himself to his people mostly in the Hebrew Language. However, because of the Gospel's special and universal message, he could not use a language that was restricted to a select few! Instead, in his providence, he waited until Alexander the Great had conquered almost all the known civilized world and had spread the Greek culture and language throughout the lands he possessed.

This was the first stage in God's plan of spreading the Gospel throughout the world. The second part involved the infamous Roman empire's powerful, resolute, and ruthless Roman Legion, who defeated the Greeks and subjugated all who opposed her. As a result, the civilized world experienced an unparalleled era of peace called the *pax Romana.* Not only did Rome bring peace to her empire, she developed a sophisticated network of roads and highways secured by her army. As a result, people could travel in safety throughout the empire. Add to all this a universal language (Greek), and you have the perfect environment in which the Gospel message could be read, taught, and promulgated throughout the world. So Jesus Christ birth was not by chance, but an inevitable event that occurred in human history when everything in the world was suited and ready for God to reveal the Gospel to mankind (Galatians 4:4).

However, even though the times and conditions made teaching and writing the Gospel possible, as time passed, defenders of biblical truth soon came to realize the necessity of using extra-biblical words to express and defend Christianity, especially the character and nature of God.

While many, even today, object to the use of words not found in the Bible to explain biblical truths and principles; the reality is that the source of the Bible is God; infinite in knowledge and wisdom, and therefore, incomprehensible to finite creatures! Regarding this statement, Dr. R. C. Sproul writes, "The purpose of technical theological language is to achieve precision of meaning as well as to safeguard the flock from cunning and subtle distortions of doctrine".[2]

In Book One of Calvin's Institutes, he expounds further on man's inability to grasp the nature of God by speaking to God's immensity and the fact that God, ". . . checks the audacity of the human mind". Both statements by Sproul and Calvin highlights the fact that if God does not speak to us in human language, his being, his grace, his mercy and his matchless love for sinners would forever remain hidden from us. Again, from Book One of Calvin's Institutes, I offer this quote, "For who is so devoid of intellect as not to understand that God, in so speaking, lisps with us as nurses are want to do with little children? Such modes of expression, therefore, do not so much express what kind of being God is, as accommodate the knowledge of him to our feebleness. In doing so, he must, of course, stoop far below his proper height". (*Institutes,* I/XIII/1)

I believe both Calvin and Dr. Sproul highlight this fact: God in his love, included as part of his predetermined plan, gifted men (especially during the early years and centuries), who were able to take and use human language to explain key concepts and truths of the Bible (cf. Ephesians 4:11-16). One such extra-biblical word is *omniscience.*

THE RELATIONSHIP BETWEEN GOD'S FOREKNOWLEDGE AND OMNISCIENCE

In order to understand God's *foreknowledge*, we must first look at how it is related to *omniscience*. First, the term *omniscience* comes from the Latin words, omni meaning all, and 'scientia' meaning knowledge. So when

---

2   Taken from *The Mystery of the Holy Spirit* by R.C. Sproul. Copyright © 1990 by R.C. Sproul. Used by permission of Tyndale House Publishers, Inc. All rights reserved.

Scripture speaks of God's *omniscience,* it means, "the absolute universality of the divine knowledge. This absolute universality is affirmed with reference to the various categories that comprise within themselves all that is possible or actual. It extends to God's own being, as well as to what exists outside of Him in the created world. God has perfect possession in consciousness of his own being". (*ISBE,* Omniscience)

He has full knowledge of everything at the same time. He knows when the smallest bird falls to the ground or how many hairs are on each head (Matthew 10:29, 30). The Hebrew writer declares all our innermost thoughts lay open and exposed before God (Hebrews 4:13). The Psalmist confesses, "Before a word is on my tongue you know it completely", (Psalms 139:4).

In the forty-sixth chapter of Isaiah, the LORD declares through the prophet Isaiah that he, "declares the end from the beginning and from ancient times the things that are not yet done" (v. 10). This verse brings out two things about God's *omniscience.* First, events or things happen not only because God knows them but because he declares them. In his wonderful book entitled, *The Attributes of God,* Arthur Pink highlights this fact in his statement, "God's knowledge does not arise from things because they are or will be but because He has ordained them to be". (Pink, *Attributes,* 22)

This is God's *omniscience,* declaring or pronouncing things, not as they occur or might happen but as they will happen because he has declared them to. Pink does not provide scriptural references for his statement, but his use of the word *'ordained'* suggests Isaiah 46:10 was in mind because the though of *ordaining* presupposes God's *omniscience* and omnipotent (all powerful).

The second fact that Isaiah 46:10 tells us about God's *omniscience* is that, because God knows everything, and knows it perfectly, he declares or ordains them before they take place. He does not need to read a book or attend classes to know the history of humanity, or the world! God determines what will be from the beginning, and the certainty of those things determined to happen is as reliable as the rising of the sun. This is seen in the words spoken by the LORD through the prophet Isaiah regarding the deliverance of Israel from Babylon, "yea, I have spoken it, I will also bring it to pass; I have purposed it, I will also do it" (Isaiah 46:11b).

God's *omniscience,* then is among the Christian's greatest assurances of his protection, provision and guidance. Jesus' words of comfort to his disciples to, ". . . take no thought, saying, What shall we eat? or, What shall we drink? or, Wherewithal shall we be clothed . . . for your heavenly Father knoweth that ye have need of all these things" (Matthew 6:31-32). No other group, Muslim, Jehovah Witness, Mormon or Buddhist has such confidence; because none of their so called gods is *omniscience* or omnipotent, and therefore, no god at all!

But how does this differ from *foreknowledge?* In other words, to know a thing beforehand is not another form of *foreknowing,* it is the same thing. If that's the case, the issue is one of semantics, not doctrine! In a sense, this is partly true and satisfies most to the point of accepting the two words as one. Rev. James M. Harrison of the Red Mills Baptist Church, shed light on this in his statement, "One cannot go to a twentieth-century English dictionary and expect to accurately discover the meaning of a first-century Greek word".[3] Though his statement is not earth shattering, sometimes the obvious is needed to help clear the fog of misunderstanding, especially regarding God's *foreknowledge.*

What then is *foreknowledge* and how are we to distinguish it from *omniscience?* First, it also is an attribute of our infinite God. As such, any hope of finite man ever understanding it adequately is dependent on God's willingness to illumine the human mind through his Spirit. After all, how is infiniteness measured? To ask the question is to speak in contradictions since a thing infinite by definition has no dimension!

This leads to the second fact regarding the question about *foreknowledge* and *omniscience; foreknowledge* is one aspect of *omniscience.* As stated previously, man is finite and a being locked in time. When he speaks about events or happenings, of necessity, it is spoken or understood from the standpoint of time. No man can claim, "Before Abraham was, I AM". God does because he is unlike His creatures that are made in time and governed by its laws. To accommodate or condescend to man, the Bible often use anthropomorphism, that is, speaking of God in human terms. *Foreknowledge* is one such anthropomorphic term signifying the aspect of

---

3   Rev. James M. Harrison, *"FOREKNOWLEDGE: There's More Than Meets God's Eye,* n.d., [http://www.redmillbaptist.org/foreknowledge.htm], (accessed September 25, 2009)

God's perfect knowledge as it relates to future things (Isaiah 41:22; 42:9; 43:9-13; 44:6-8; 46:10; Daniel 2:22; Amos 3:7).

God is *omniscience* and because he is, he *foreknows* the future. God knows everything perfectly, not as fortune-tellers, psychics, or prophets claim to know; but because he is *omniscience!* Any other aspect of how we are to understand this glorious attribute of God is to destroy the essence of what makes him who he is: all wise, all knowing, and all seeing.

Foreknowledge and its Relationship to Foreordination

Another crucial term worth looking at in regards to our election is, *foreordination.* In a way, God's *foreknowledge* is based on his *foreordination.* In other words, he knows what will take place beforehand because he has *ordained* and decreed it to take place. As such, he *foreknows.* Put another way, God's *foreknowledge* is his perfect knowledge of what he knows will take place while his *foreordination* is the outworking of that knowledge. (*ISBE,* Foreknow; Foreknowledge)

This is not a difficult concept as we do it every day when making plans for a vacation or our agenda for a given period of time. This is *foreordination* on a finite scale, the difference being found in the key word finite. In other words, we make plans, to do this or that, on tomorrow or move to a different city on a given date; however our success in all these areas always lies in the realm of possibility, not certainty! I may become terminally ill or lose my job. These are but two things that may or may not change my original plan. However, when it comes to God's ordained plan, there is nothing or no one that can stop it from coming to pass.

Take, for example, the Old Testament story of Joseph's brothers selling him into slavery (which will be discussed again in the chapter on predestination). At the time, his brothers' had no idea they were part of a greater plan. Even poor Jacob, when making the coat of many colors, was totally unaware of God's comprehensive plan for him, his family and the future nation called Israel! Now, did God simply foresee Jacob and his son's actions ahead of time and then design his plan around them?

Think of God's dilemma in that scenario. Jacob might have seen the error of favoring Joseph over his older brothers and not made the coat at all. A greater scenario has the brothers actually killing their younger brother. Far fetch? Not really, since their jealous and malignant heart had seriously entertained the idea (Genesis 37:4; Genesis 37:20).

These examples prove God is not, as theists insist, just a spectator in his creation. He *foreordained* how His creation would bring glory to him. This does not mean humanity, and all other creatures are puppets acting at the whim of a capricious God whose only motive is self-satisfaction. Nothing is further from the truth. While nothing happens in God's creation apart from His *foreordination*, people still acts freely, so that although God *foreordains* and *foreknows*, man is still held accountable for his actions.

While seemingly a contradiction, Scriptures makes it clear that everyone will stand before God to give an account of what they have done in this life (2 Corinthians 5:10; Revelation 20:13). Therefore, *foreordination* and *foreknowledge* are not contradictions but mysteries God has not chosen to fully reveal. Therefore, we glory in the God of grace and his matchless love; who *foreordained* us unto salvation.

QUESTIONS TO PONDER

1. How is God's sovereignty related to omniscience, foreknowledge and foreordination?
2. Why must we always look at God's foreknowledge from the standpoint of His love?
3. How has this chapter helped your understanding of God's Omniscience and foreknowledge?
4. Has this chapter helped you better understand God's total involvement in your salvation?
5. Many Christians believe they can lose their salvation. How does Jesus' declaration that no one 'can' come to Him unless the Father draws them help your understanding of the 'security' of a person's salvation?

CHAPTER 8

God's Foreknowledge

The previous chapter looked at the relationship between *foreknowledge, omniscience* and *foreordination*; three fundamental doctrines needed for a proper understanding of *election* and ultimately our salvation. This was necessary to establish a foundation to begin this next aspect of *foreknowledge* as used in the New Testament.

Again, this book and a hundred more like it will never bring the camps of those who believe in man's autonomy and those who believe in God's sovereignty in salvation; nor is it the author's intent. Instead, the book's goal is to encourage many more Christians to become like the Bereans mentioned in Acts 17:11; who searched the Scriptures for themselves in order to avoid falling victim to false teachings. Having this mindset about the Scripture allows the Holy Spirit to remove the scales of 'ism' from our spirit, and we become like Saul of Tarsus, enabled to see God as never before. This is the author's purpose and prayer.

Having said that, let's return to our discussion on *foreknowledge.* It is fascinating to note that when the word *foreknowledge* is examined, we find that its use is rare in the New Testament. Strong's Concordance narrows its use, or some derivative of it, to only five: two in Romans, one in Acts, and one in Peter's first letter. However, like many other foundational doctrines of the Christian faith, its essence lies within the context. In other words, a proper studying of the context, along with its supporting passages, brings out its doctrinal truths. Failure to go further than its common use, even when clearly understood, deprives the Believer of a proper understanding of God's infinite love and the fact that salvation is wholly of God.

With that in mind, let's look at how the first century reader and writer, especially Paul, understood and used this term. As stated earlier, when discussing God's *foreknowledge, prescience* (foresight or insight) is usually in view. While this reasoning is correct, biblical and necessary; the concept itself is the exception and not the norm in the New Testament. In other words, *foreknowledge* focuses on God's sovereignty and his wondrous love for the elect.

FOREKNOWLEDGE AND GOD'S SOVEREIGNTY

There is no denial that *foreknowledge* is also at the heart of *prescience*, but in the author's opinion, *foreknowledge,* as used in the New Testament, manifests God's love more directly, more thoroughly and more visibly. This is especially true when the facets of redemption are examined and laid out. *Foreknowledge* personifies God's love in a way unimaginable to our thoughts and incomprehensible in our thinking. Who among us can properly understand how and why a holy God did what he did, just to save; not righteous people, or even people seeking him or his will for them; but evil, vile, and despicable people! Yet, these are the exact kinds of people God directed His love; enemies who loathed him, his ways, his laws, and his person!

Having said all that, this begs the question, "How does *foreknowledge* help our understanding of this great, or as the songwriter states, amazing love of God"? To answer this question, we start with this first fact about *foreknowledge:* its definition. In the New Testament, *foreknowledge* is translated from two Greek words meaning *forethought* or *foreseen.* Contextually, both words focus more on God's *foreordination* than his *prescience.* Take, for example, Peter's words in that great sermon on the Day of Pentecost, "Him, being delivered by the determinate counsel and foreknowledge of God, ye have taken, and by wicked hands have crucified and slain" (Acts 2:23, my emphasis added*).*

Why did the Jews turn Jesus over to Pilate for crucifixion? Though their actions were their own, they were not isolated from the *'determinate counsel'* and God's *foreknowledge* according to this passage. Again, though *prescience* is inherent in the statement, it is not Peter's primary focus nor is it the idea behind the Greek word translated *foreknowledge* in Acts 2:23. Instead, the use of *foreknowledge* in this verse emphasize the fact that the actions taken by the Jews against Jesus was part of God's 'fixed plan', that is, God had 'perfect foresight of all the steps involved in it'. (*ISBE,* Foreknow; Foreknowledge)

The Holy Spirit highlights this truth of God's foresight in the latter part of the verse, where he declares, "ye have taken, and by wicked hands have crucified and slain" (Acts. 23b). Notice the emphasis placed on individual responsibility, 'ye have taken'. They had taken him from the garden! They had brought and accused him before the Sanhedrin and Pilate! They cried and demanded his crucifixion! All was done by their own volition without coercion from any outside force because their actions were a reflection of their evil nature. Therefore, the guilt was theirs and theirs alone. God simply withheld his divine grace by not restraining them; thus, leaving them to their own evil intentions and desires.

The passage in Acts reveals more clearly the fact that oftentimes when *foreknowledge* is used in the New Testament, it is much closer to God's *foreordination*. The Holy Spirit highlights this principle by declaring that God's *foreknowledge* is based on God's '*determinate counsel*'.

No two words, are more pertinent when discussing '*foreknowledge*' than these two; *determinate* and *counsel*. *Determinate* comes from a Greek word meaning, something marked out or bounded. Today, when a farmer or landowner wants to identify his property, he puts up a fence or some other parameter to mark or identify it as his own. This is the idea behind this word and how Peter's audience would have understood it. Also, implicit in this word is the idea of purpose as indicated by its use in Acts 11:29 where the disciples determined (the same Greek word) to send relief to the Church at Judea.

So when Peter speaks of the *determinate counsel*, he has in mind God's intended purpose and plan regarding the death of his son and the role played not only by the Jews in general, but in particular; the Sanhedrin Council, Pilate, Herod, and Judas. Therefore, what took place at Calvary, along with all the events leading up to it, were 'marked off' by God; not at that time but before the foundation of the world. God *foreordained* and decreed it all! Jesus' death was not unforeseen by God, but *determined* by Him!

Counsel is another fascinating word that is unique to the New Testament. When we think of *counsel*, the thought of someone receiving advice from another comes to mind. However, the Greek word translated *counsel* in Acts 2:23 means much more than that, for who can advise God of anything! Regarding the definition of this word, John Gill writes, "It expresses the act of the mind in willing, or the purpose or design which is formed". (John Gill, *John Gill's Exposition*, Acts 2:23)

Taken together then, these two words highlights God's *foreordained* plan of delivering Jesus to the proper authorities for crucifixion. Because this plan was fixed or marked out by God and in agreement with his will and purpose, the actions involved were in accordance with the *foreknowledge* of God. This reality along with Peter's further explanation of all that was behind the death, burial and resurrection of Jesus Christ, is what drove the people to cry out, "What shall we do" (Acts 2:37). So then, this passage helps us understand *foreknowledge,* as used in the New Testament, as meaning God's *foreordination* or his knowledge of his own eternal purpose.

The other question that always comes up in God's *foreordination* is the idea of free-will. In other words, if God has foreordained an event, how can he hold those involved in it accountable and responsible. Like many, this issue has and continues to be a mystery and therefore, any comments on my part are not only futile, but fruitless! I, along with others, who are much more knowledgeable and qualified in this subject, choose to remain silent on this issue and instead delight in God's wisdom to act upon those whom he has elected in this way!

FOREKNOWLEDGE AND GOD'S ETERNAL RELATIONSHIP WITH THE ELECT

Looking at *foreknowledge* from the perspective of *prescience* and *foreordination* was essential in bringing out the greatness and glory of God's *foreknowledge* as it relates to our salvation. For while it could be said, He *foresaw* our expression of faith in His Son, it can never be said that that expression of faith was the result of our ability or volition. In other words, the faith exercised in believing Jesus Christ as Savior is not something that originates in the human heart, but is given to us by God Himself (Ephesians 2:8). This act done on the part of God is another manifestation of his *foreknowledge* and at the same time stress God's sovereign will acting on the passive object. Any other belief or teaching regarding the role of God's foreknowledge in our salvation is totally unscriptural and must be rejected. As Pink writes, such false theology, ". . . makes God's foreknowledge of our believing the cause of His election to salvation; whereas, God's election is the cause, and our believing in Christ is the effect" (Pink, *Attributes*, 23).

From the standpoint of salvation, *foreknowledge* is not just God's *foreordination* or even his *prescience*; it goes further because it is grounded in an intimate relationship established by him before 'the foundations of the world' with those chosen to be saved (Ephesians 1:4). The best way to understand this statement is not to rely on the definition given earlier, as that definition's focus was God's *foreordination*. However, as it relates to salvation, *foreknowledge* seldom, if ever has reference to events that are yet to happen.

Perhaps it is better to look at the word '*know*' and its use in both the Old and New Testament. A careful study of this word reveals that it always has reference to God's relationship with his people (cf. Ex. 33:17; Deut. 9:24; Jer. 1:5; Hos. 8:4; Amos 3:2; Matthew 7:23; John 10:14; 1 Corinthian 8:3; 2 Timothy 2:19). In all instances, the word signifies either, "loved or appointed". A closer study reveals that it does not simply denotes a casual relationship, but an affection for the object in view. So deep is the affection implied in this word that it is used of sexual relations as in "Adam knew Eve'. When combined with *'fore'*, it heightens the significance of this relationship by stressing that it did not begin at the point of salvation, but according to the Apostle Paul, it began before time (Ephesians 1:4; 2 Thessalonians 2:13).

Finally, Paul writes, "And we know that all things work together for good to them that love God, to them who are the called according to his purpose. For whom he did foreknow, he also did predestinate to be conformed to the image of his Son, that he might be the firstborn among many brethren" (Romans 8:28-29). The central truth of that passage is God's work on behalf of the sinner; 'he' called, he *foreknew*, and he predestinated. Perhaps Pink summed the whole concept of foreknowledge up in these words, "The fact is that 'foreknowledge' is never used in Scripture in connection with events or actions; instead, it always has reference to persons. It is persons God is said to "foreknow," not the actions of those persons". (Pink, *Attributes*, 24) Let those of us who were *foreknown* by God rest in this reality; our salvation is secure, not because we first loved him but because he first loved us and established a relationship with us before the foundation of the world!

QUESTIONS TO PONDER

1. How do you understand the relationship between God's omniscience and His foreknowledge?

2. If God knows everything that we're going to do before we do it, why doesn't He stop us from doing bad things? Does this make God Himself evil?

3. Has this chapter given you a better understanding of the Jews' role in the events leading up to the crucifixion of Jesus? Explain your answer in light of situations in your own life and your understanding of God's determinate counsel.

4. How has this chapter helped your understanding of God's love for us? What impact has it has on your commitment to serve Him?

CHAPTER 9

Predestination

God's foreknowledge, as is true of all his attributes, magnifies his grace and mercy. However, it does not stand alone but is a facet of another critical doctrine of Christianity known as *predestination*. Think about this truth for a moment! God establishes an everlasting relationship, not with angels mind you, but human beings who, according to the Psalmist, are made a little lower than angels! Add to this, the fact that he established this relationship with people whose existence rested entirely within his mind. In other words, though we had no existence in time, God saw all of us, not just as part of his creation,; but our eventual fall through Adam, our subsequent need of a Savior, our justification, sanctification and ultimately our glorification (Romans 8:28-30).

Some might ask, "If God saw all that beforehand, why didn't he change it or just create us and take us to heaven"! Although, it's not possible to go to a particular passage and get an exact answer to that particular question, Christians find confidence in Paul's words to the Ephesians, that all this was done, "according to the good pleasure of his will" (Ephesians 1:5). Paul's emphasis in those words is the fact that, God's glory is the sole reason and cause of all his acts of grace and compassion towards Christians and non-Christians. This again highlights John Newton's summation of God's grace; it is amazing!

Though this answer is rather simplistic, it lies at the heart of why God saves some and passes over others. As stated earlier, we are not saved by anything we do, or because we are born into a Christian household; instead as Paul emphasize in his letter to the church at Ephesus, it is, "by grace, that no man might boast" (Ephesians 2:8).

Inherent in all human beings is the desire to be the master of their own destiny, especially when it comes to their eternal destination. Foreknowledge helps us understand that our helplessness brought about by the sin force's power over us makes it necessary for God active involvement in the total process of salvation. If left to our own devices and wisdom, it is certain that none of us would ever turn to Jesus Christ for salvation. Therefore, God set in place a predetermined course, unique and specific, for each person elected by him. This wonderful plan is called *predestination* and is the focus of this chapter.

THE SIGNIFICANCE OF PREDESTINATION

Besides election, there is perhaps no other doctrine that is so misunderstood, denied, and neglected than *predestination*. The reason for the problems surrounding both doctrines is traceable to preconceived ideas and a misunderstanding of its use in Greek culture. Since the latter is the most significant cause, it's better to start there; once clarity is arrived and agreed upon there, hopefully, the former will become a logical conclusion.

First of all, *Predestination* comes from two Greek words: *pro* meaning before and *horizo* meaning to limit. Though both words are needed in bringing the reader or student to a proper understanding, it is *horizo* that brings out more clearly what is in view when *predestination* is used in Scripture because it transliterates over into the English word horizon.

This is an important fact in understanding *predestination* and how it relates to salvation. In other words, when we hear or read the word horizon, it conjures up in the mind a picture that seemingly has the ocean and sky merging as one. Obviously this is not the case, but that's the sense gathered from the word, or when we're looking out in the distance from a ship sailing on the ocean. The only way to either eliminate or understand this idea would be for the viewer to sail to the end of the ocean.

That's the idea behind these two Greek words translated in Scripture as *predestination*. God beforehand fixed a boundary around those whom he elected to guarantee our salvation and ultimate glorification! Therefore, nothing can happen to those elected by God that would prevent their salvation and its ultimate goal: glorification. God has so fixed this boundary that even our own recklessness, mistakes, and even the evil intentions of others cannot affect it one way or the other. Furthermore, nothing happens in the life of the elect, even before they're saved, that is outside this *predetermined* parameter (see image on next page).

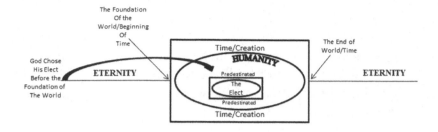

Predestination: A Fixed Boundary Around God's Elect

AN ILLUSTRATION OF PREDESTINATION FROM THE OLD TESTAMENT

Perhaps the greatest illustration of this doctrine is seen in the life of Joseph. Hated and despised by his brothers and eventually sold to slave traders, Joseph ended up in the household of Egypt's Captain of the Guard (Genesis 39:1). The outsider looking in on this scenario would undoubtedly see only victory for the brothers, just as they deduced.

But the brothers' deduction was incorrect since they had no idea their actions were within God's predetermined plan, not only for their brother Joseph, but their's and their father. They could not see that Joseph would one day be elevated to an influential position within the Egyptian government. As far as they were concerned, selling their brother to slave-traders was the end of the matter.

Do you see the *horizo?* Let's follow the sequence of events in God's predetermined plan; Joseph being handed over to slave-traders, his subsequent imprisonment and ultimately his appointment as a leader within the Egyptian government. As discussed in the previous chapter on foreknowledge, God *predetermined* all those events, yet all the players and events were designed to achieve one thing for Joseph, one thing for the Egyptians and yet another for the Hebrew people. As such, not a single event could have happened any other way than it did.

Imagine what would have happened if the brothers original plan had succeeded. Joseph would never have reached Egypt and therefore, never interacted with all the players needed to get him in a position to advise Pharaoh. As a result, the famine would have taken a devastating toll on the Egyptian regime; and more importantly, destroyed Joseph and his family.

It is the latter that carries the greatest importance because from that family, came the nation Israel and the Savior of the world!

However, it did not go the way of man but remained within boundaries set by a supreme, sovereign and almighty God. Joseph's brothers acts, while their own, were part of God's *predestined* plan. That's why Joseph comforted his brothers later with these words, "for God did send me before you to preserve life" (Genesis 45:5).

PREDESTINATION ALWAYS HAS AS ITS FOCUS A SPECIFIC PEOPLE AND END

Israel's history reveals another critical aspect of *predestination.* It always has as its object those elected or chosen by God. Scripture never speaks of the unsaved as being predestined to be unsaved or predestined to go to hell. Instead, as Dr. Dwight W. Pentecost points out, this word "is always qualified by a statement of the end or aim in view". (Pentecost, *Sound Doctrine*, 141)

That aim relates to what God is doing for and through his people in salvation. According to the first chapter of Paul's book to the Church at Ephesus, God's purpose behind *predestination* is to make us heirs through adoption (vv. 4-5, 11). The reality of this goal could never come to fruition without God's direct involvement in the lives of sinners who were incapable of affecting their wretched condition.

But the greatest end or purpose of *predestination* is given to us in the eighth chapter of Romans where Paul tells us that God predestined us "to be conformed to the image of his Son" (v.29). This ultimate goal helps us understand why God must establish parameters for our lives to ensure his divine purpose is achieved. Again, *predestination* is not done in a capricious manner. God in his own way and for his own purpose has determined and purposed that some would become sons of glory (I Corinthians 2:7). In doing so, he does not override our volition but works within it in a way incomprehensible and unknown to us. It is one of God's greatest mysteries and a magnificent display of divine love.

Off course, the obvious question by most at this point is, "How can God condemn anyone justly, if he has not *predestined* or chosen them"? To that age old question, the Spirit gives this answer, "Therefore, hath he mercy on whom he will have mercy" (Romans 9:18). As discussed in a previous chapter of this book, God was under no obligation to bestow mercy on any of us, since we all were guilty through our father Adam and fitted for destruction. If God had chosen not to save one single person, not only would he have been justified in doing so, but no one would have had grounds for rebuttal or complaint!

Instead, he chose to show mercy, not on all, but on some. Therefore, the question becomes, who among men would deny God the same basic freedom of choice allowed to the typical consumer who selects two or three apples out from among others simply because they chose to do so, or simply because it pleased them?

As stated in a previous chapter, such illustrations describes to a limited degree God's choice of certain people from the one common mass of humanity. With this in mind, the Christian must also conclude, that boasting on our part is excluded when it comes to our salvation, since we were totally passive in this and all aspects of salvation. The Christian who does not understand and cherish this fundamental truth has not fully come to terms with the grace of God or their salvation!

QUESTIONS TO PONDER

1. In your own words, define predestination.
2. How has this chapter helped your understanding of predestination?
3. As you looked back over your life, can you see evidences of God's predestination. List as many as you can think of.

CHAPTER 10

You Must Be Born Again:
The Role of the Holy Spirit

W hen looking back on our lives, one question often pondered is, "How did I escape that tragedy in my life"? This varies from the bullet that just missed to a deadly illness. What made it all possible? The unbeliever and sadly, some Christians, accredit 'lady luck' or finally conclude it to be purely coincidental.

However, those who fully understand God's predestined plan see his loving care in all such events, shielding and protecting those whom he has chosen to be saved. His purpose is to ensure their arrival at his appointed time when he calls them out of sin's *darkness* into his marvelous *light* of salvation. These three words: *darkness, call* and *light* are key words in our understanding of why salvation is wholly of God.

All three highlights the reason why it must be so! As emphasized in the third chapter of this book, man is lost and totally separated from God. His realm is not only one of death (separation from God), but is characterized by acts of darkness and evil. One cannot expect anything less from beings whose hearts are enveloped in darkness. This is the reason these three words were chosen and must be examined.

MAN'S PROBLEM: HE LIVES IN DARKNESS AND VANITY

Notice this first word, *darkness*. When talking about the purpose of Jesus coming into the world, the Apostle John declares Him to be, "the true Light, which lighteth every man that cometh into the world" (John 1:9). The truth declared in this verse is, all of humanity is born into *darkness*, and that darkness so overwhelms it that every act, every thought, and every desire is tainted by it. Even the supposed good deeds are dark and evil because they originate within a heart and mind totally controlled by *darkness*!

The Apostle Paul helps our understanding of this condition in the fourth chapter of his letter to the Church at Ephesus. Notice how he describes the life of the Christian prior to being saved,

> This I say therefore, and testify in the Lord, that ye henceforth walk not as other Gentiles walk, in the vanity of their mind, Having the understanding darkened, being alienated from the life of God through the ignorance that is in them, because of the blindness of their heart: Who being past feeling have given themselves over unto lasciviousness, to work all uncleanness with greediness. (Ephesians 4:17b-19)

The first thing taught in this passage about man in *darkness* is; his *mind* or outlook on life is characterized by *vanity*. First, let's look at the term, *mind*. When used in Scripture (especially in the New Testament), this word carries two meanings: one deals with the whole person while the second deals with the person's intellect, will, and conscience. In this passage from Ephesians chapter four, the latter definition is in view.

How often have we read or heard on the news about behaviors that seem to defy human logic? Whether it's the exploitation of children, the senseless drive-by shootings, robberies perpetrated on the most innocent of victims and on and on the list could go. Such actions sprang from an uninformed conscience directed by an intellect and will, ignorant of the knowledge of God's commandments. This is not just one of the reasons for man's shocking and immoral behavior, it is the leading cause!

No place is this idea brought out more clearly than in the seventh chapter of Paul's letter to the Romans. In that chapter, Paul describes man as wanting to do right, that is, wanting to be a good husband, son or brother. However, the reality is that, evil overcomes every effort (Romans 7:15, 18-20). Paul concludes that a principle is at work in him; one so powerful and absolute that it always leads a person to do the very thing he hates. This principle or force so dominates our whole being through our nature, that Paul likens it to a slave-master! As the governing law of master of our soul, it controls and directs the mind, which in turn controls the will and conscience. From our previous discussion, we know this force to be sin.

This brings us to the second word, vanity. Usually when we think of vain, the immediate though is self-centeredness. However, its use in the seventeenth verse of Ephesians chapter four is quite different. It comes from the Greek word *mataiotes (mat-ah-yot-ace)*. In their commentary, *Jamieson, Faussett and Brown* summarize the meaning of this word as, "the waste of the rational powers on worthless objects". (*JFB*, Ephesians 4:17) Based on their definition, this word seems to highlight the effects of an unregenerate mind, that is, its affections and desires are directed towards worthless objects.

GOD'S CALL

From this hopeless state of *darkness* and vanity, God calls or *summon* the sinner! Here, is the mystery and grandeur of salvation; mainly God's *call* to undeserving and wretched people from the realm of *darkness*. God must invade the sinner's realm of reality and bring about a radical change to their situation! As slaves to their sin-nature, they cannot act nor respond to God's gift of salvation unless he takes the initiative (Ephesians 2:3-4).

We looked at this term call earlier during our discussion in chapter five regarding Abraham's election. As pointed out then, this call is more than a summon; it is God's inward work within the sinner where he supernaturally changes their disposition towards Him. In other words, he changes their mind by enlightening it towards his grace, love and mercy. In doing so, he removes *vanity* from us and sets our mind and heart upon Christ as the object of our love and adoration.

When this happens, the sinner sees his vileness and cries out to God to save him! This is the effect of God's call, which is commonly referred to as his effectual call. The added term, effectual highlights the fact that those whom God calls will always respond, not from coercion, but because of the radical change brought about within their soul by God.

This is a hard saying and undoubtedly one hard to accept. But hopefully after reading the chapters up to this point, the reader must know of a certainty, that freedom from one's sin-nature is impossible, since it is as much a part of us as our own breath! No amount of research groups, workshops, treatment centers or any other such man-made solutions can solve this problem! The sinner's only hope is God's effectual call on their life. A call so great, so powerful and so efficacious that it snatches and draws the sinner out of the realm of *darkness* and *vanity* into His Kingdom!

What Brings About This Call

We see the supernatural nature of this effectual call in Jesus' response to Nicodemus, "Ye must be born again" (John 3:3,7). This seemingly impossible, but necessary act (of being born again) even puzzled Nicodemus, who was also a Jewish teacher! Hear the bewilderment in his response to Jesus' declaration, "How can a man be born when he is old? Can he enter the second time into his mother's womb, and be born" (John 3:4)?

Is that not still the question of the sinner? If this act requires a rebirth, how is it possible? What is the process? That's the dilemma! In other words, even if the hypothesis is accepted, it only serves to highlight the futility of the conflict and cast the person further into a chasm of hopelessness!

But thank God, Jesus does not leave Nicodemus to ponder this question but helps him understand that the new birth he's talking about is not physical, but spiritual. Realizing Nicodemus', and any human being for that matter, difficulty in comprehending his statement, Jesus uses the illustration of a physical birth to help Nicodemus' understanding.

His point to Nicodemus was that the Kingdom of Heaven is not physical, but spiritual; it is not of this world. However, though it is spiritual, it operates under the same principles as the physical world. In other words, the fetus remains in the womb and separated from the physical world until a physical birth takes place! This same principle is just as applicable to being born in the spiritual Kingdom of God: a person must be born into it (see image on next page)!

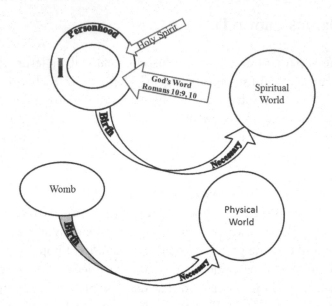

The Physical Birth Explains the Necessity of The Spiritual Birth

However, to Nicodemus and any clearly thinking person, the idea of being reborn is not only illogical but humanly speaking, impossible. But as difficult as it seems, Jesus' words to Nicodemus and the world remains, "Marvel not that I said unto thee, Ye must be born again" (John 3:7). This key doctrinal statement sets forth a significant distinction between Christianity and religion!

Christians are not people attempting to make themselves morally right or holy through virtuous deeds, philosophy or written rules, or writings of one person or counsel. Instead, as stated so humbly by Martin Luther, we are 'aliens'! Though we exist in this physical world our real existence resides in the spiritual realm. Put another way, any righteous act or deed claimed by Christians is not theirs by nature, but is the manifestation of the nature of Jesus Christ, of which we are but a partner (2 Peter 1:4)!

But I digress. Let us return to Nicodemus' original question, "How can one be born again"? The answer lies in the example given of the physical birth; just as two agents are needed to bring it about, so are two agents involved in the new birth. Jesus identifies these agents as ' . . . water' and 'the Spirit' (John 3:5). Some translates this verse as "water, even the Spirit", indicating that *water* and *spirit* are synonymous.

Again, neither translations detract from the meaning of Christ's words to Nicodemus, as will be shown later in this and the next chapter. The main point, and emphasis of the current discussion between Jesus and Nicodemus is to highlight the fact that, if you want to become part of the spiritual realm, you must be born into it! To help our understanding, he cites another vital principle of birth: "That which is born of the flesh is flesh; and that which is born of the Spirit is spirit" (John 3:6).

Jesus' words highlight the fundamental principle that like begets like (John 1:12, 13). Therefore, it is clear that a new-birth is needed to take us out of our current realm of reality into the spiritual realm. Refusal to accept this basic fact is not only a state of denial but foolish!

THE MYSTERY OF THE NEW BIRTH

But again, how does it take place? By *water* and the *spirit*! As stated earlier, since the Holy Spirit is the subject of the discussion between Christ and Nicodemus, some take both terms as meaning the same thing (and that may well be). However, this chapter's objective is not to give a full exposition of the passage but to point out the necessity of the active agents involved. In other words, natural birth is not self-generated, but results from an act initiated by a man and a woman.

That principle is just as true in the spiritual realm. The only difference is the process and agents involved. God the Father initiates and brings about this new birth through the *Holy Spirit*. This is the meaning behind Jesus' words, "that which is born of the Spirit is spirit", and is another key difference between Christianity and religion.

The relationship shared between Jesus Christ and Christians is not only based on trust and truths about his person, redemptive work, and teachings; it is also the result of being made a part of him through this new birth. As such, we become so much a part of his life and nature, that all Christians, both alive and dead, are regarded as comprising the body of Christ (John 15:1-7; I Corinthians 12:13; Ephesians 1:23).

The Apostle Paul highlights this relationship or union in his letter to the Galatians in these words, ". . . nevertheless I live; yet not I, but Christ liveth in me: and the life which I now live in the flesh I live by the faith of the Son of God, who loved me, and gave himself for me" (2:20). This fact is not true of any other religion or group in the world, either then or now!

The union between Jesus Christ and His people is a mystery, and even though we speak of a new realm, it is more than that! Christians are actually part of a new life whose existence is in a new realm commonly referred to in the New Testament as the body of Christ, the Kingdom of Heaven or the Kingdom of God. It is spiritual and not physical; therefore, in order to become part of it, a person must be spiritually born into it!

This is what Jesus was explaining to Nicodemus; that which is born naturally can only produce beings in the natural realm. As such, they are controlled by the principles and laws governing it. The inhabitants of the natural realm can no more change their behavior than a fish can expect to live out of its natural habitation. If a change is to occur, either the realm of existence must change or the person themselves. The impossibility of the latter highlights Jesus' words, "Ye must be born" into the spiritual realm since, "that which is born of the Spirit is spirit".

This whole process or transition from the natural into the spiritual comes about through the work and supernatural power of the *Holy Spirit*. He does not seek permission nor is his work thwarted by the weakness or unwillingness of man any more than the child born through natural birth. Again, listen to the Scripture's account in the first chapter of the Gospel of John regarding this process, Jesus seems to go out of his way to emphasize that those who believe in him are those, "Which were born, not of blood, nor of the will of the flesh, nor of the will of man, but of God" (John 1:12-13).

Do you see the similarity? Just as a child's generation normally results from the conscience and willing decisions between a man and woman; so one is born into the spiritual realm by the active will of God the Father through the *Holy Spirit*. If God's spirit does not act on the deadened and darkened soul of the sinner, then not one single person would ever be saved!

The persistent attitude of the unsaved person regarding their ability to change themselves and accept Christ on their own, is attributable to the failure of drawing a distinction between the natural and spiritual birth.

As stated previously, natural science dictates that human conception is the result of someone else's willful act. Without this initial process, birth is impossible! This is just as true of the spiritual birth; the object is entirely passive and unaware of what is happening! Therefore, we concluded that the first agent of the new birth and the call of God is the *Holy Spirit*!

QUESTIONS TO PONDER

1. Why must we always see ourselves from God's perspective when we talk about salvation?
2. How does the word darkness help your understanding of why people act as they do?
3. In reading about the discussion of Jesus' conversation with Nicodemus in this chapter, has it enhanced your understanding of man's inability to save himself? How has this affected your view of "Once saved, always saved"?

CHAPTER 11

The Second Agent of the New Birth:
The Role of God's Word

The previous chapter established the need for the new birth as well as the fact it is not by one's own ability but is made possible by two agents. The first one being the Holy Spirit! In this chapter, we will endeavor to identify and understand the second agent, identified by the term *water* in the third chapter of John's Gospel.

Space does not allow an elaboration on the various schools of thoughts, nor is it the author's intention to present such arguments. Instead, the focus here is to help those truly seeking understanding in this matter to discover what the word of God declares about this subject. To this end, only passages dealing with this subject clearly will be considered. This does not mean that controversial passages are any less valuable or that we should avoid them. Instead, it highlights the principle that difficult passages must be interpreted in light of related passages dealing with the same teaching that are clearer, or less controversial.

THE MEANS OF CONFESSING JESUS CHRIST AS LORD

The first passage is Romans 10:9-10, which not only completes the picture given by Christ to Nicodemus, but also identify the second agent of the new birth. According to those two verses, a person must do three things in order to be born into this new realm. First, they must confess with their mouth the Lord Jesus.

At the outset, the point must be stressed; this is more than just verbalizing, "I believe in Jesus Christ"! In other words, many people believe Jesus Christ lived and died, yet they remain in the realm of darkness and vanity! Additionally, Scripture declares that Satan not only believes in

Christ, but trembles from such belief (James 2:19). So obviously, there is more in view here than just believing intellectually.

The key to understanding the meaning behind this phrase is found in the little word confess; meaning to agree with what someone else has said. So, elemental in this first step is an agreement to something or with someone. The 'something' is the acknowledgment that Jesus Christ is Lord.

Normally, when we think of this term Lord, what comes to mind is the lordship of Christ, and of necessity that must be included. However, when Paul talks about Lord in the tenth chapter of Romans, he has in mind Christ's divinity or the fact that Jesus Christ is God! Therefore, the first step in the process of salvation is agreement with Scripture that Jesus Christ is God.

Unfortunately, we live in a society and culture that devalues and place Jesus Christ, not simply on the same level as other religious figures, but puts him in their shadows. One need only look at the intolerance and ridicule waged against him on a daily basis. Yet, according to Paul, or better yet, the Holy Spirit, the rebirth is not possible apart from this initial confession. There are absolutely no exceptions! Even the Jew must make the confession that the same Jesus, who they and their fathers and forefathers rejected, is God! Otherwise; they face the same fate of the Gentiles they so despise (John 8:31-58).

Perhaps, no one in the first century hated Jesus more than his own people, even the Apostle Paul initially. Their hatred centered, not around the fact that he was bad or evil, or that his deeds or intentions were bad; but simply because he claimed to be the Son of God!

But note Paul's further emphasis; this confession is with the mouth. On the surface, this appears to be a redundant statement since any nonverbal confession is regarded as worthless by any standard. However, I believe Paul's reasoning is grounded in the nature and character of his contemporary audience. Remember, these were Jews—for them, even today—to confess Jesus Christ as God was the height of blasphemy, and therefore unthinkable!

Here were these particular people, who according to Paul were "Israelites; to whom pertaineth the adoption" (Romans 9:4). This meant they were chosen out from among all the nations of the world to become the people of God. They were a holy people whose fathers had enjoyed the blessings, protection and deliverance of God in every respect. So unique are they to God that he says to the enemies of Israel, "he that toucheth you toucheth the apple of his eye" (Zechariah 2:8).

Not only are they the physical family of God, but Paul reminds them of the fact that God had revealed himself to them in a way he has never done for any other people (cf. Romans 9:4-5). One of the best examples is his presence with them after their deliverance from Egypt in the pillar of cloud by day and a pillar of fire by night (Exodus 32:21, 22).

They knew he existed and that his love for them was different and special. He demonstrated this through the covenant made with Abraham, Isaac, Jacob, Moses and David. And while these blessings were great, the greatest blessing of all was the promise of a deliverer who would be greater than Moses and even greater than their greatest king, David! He would crush their enemies and restore Israel to its former greatness.

No other people had this privilege of having their God come, live, and perform mighty signs and wonders before them! Only they knew that Emanuel (meaning God with us) would be born; not as a Roman, or a Greek, or Egyptian, but a Jew! Yet, when he came, they denied, rejected and turned him over to the Romans to be killed in the most brutal way!

What is the point of all this? To simply point out that if the Jews (with all their knowledge of God; his special relationship with them and the fact his Son was born from their roots) has to confess Jesus Christ as God, then how much more is this true of all other people? This is why I believe, in his infinite wisdom, God placed these verses in connection with the Jews; his privileged and chosen people.

Not only does the confession involve acknowledging Jesus Christ as God, one must also agree that God raised him from the dead through the power of the Holy Spirit. These two truths are foundational to the Christian faith; along with the virgin birth of Jesus Christ, they both set Christianity apart from any group in the world!

While world religions have their leaders and adhere to their moral and philosophical teachings, none can make the same claims about them as the Christian can about Jesus Christ. And even those who do so have no credible evidence that would stand the test of authenticity, time, or history. Only Christianity can provide evidence about Christ's birth, life, death, and resurrection so conclusive and verifiable that all efforts by man to refute it, has and will always fail!

The Confession of Jesus Christ as Lord Made Possible by Faith

But how is man able to come to such knowledge, or as Paul declares, ". . . how shall they believe in him of whom they have not heard" (Romans 10:14, my emphasis)? On the surface, this rhetorical question seems illogical; since it's obvious that belief is impossible apart from having knowledge of the thing, or in this case, the person in whom one believes. So why raise the issue at all?

The first reason for doing so is to highlight the spiritual nature of the confession. In other words, in view is not just a person's physical hearing, since nearly everyone in the world has heard about Jesus Christ, but something much greater. Remember, the basis of this whole discussion is to disclose the identity of the other agent involved in God's effectual call and the subsequent new birth that gets a person into the kingdom of God.

In doing so, the significance of the Jews and their relationship with God was brought to the forefront to show that even they needed the new birth. However, in order for them to partake of it, confession of Jesus Christ as Lord was necessary.

If anyone knew about Jesus Christ in Paul's day, it was the Jews. After all, Paul was one himself! They had not only heard of him, many lived during the time of Paul's letter to the Romans and probably witnessed or may have played an active role in Jesus' crucifixion. All this is said to highlight the fact that it is not enough to simply hear or read about Jesus Christ, if one expects to experience the rebirth.

Another reason and perhaps the greatest one, is brought out in the phrase, "believe in him". The emphasis here is that after hearing about Jesus Christ, one has to 'believe in him', or put their complete trust and confidence in him and his work. This leads us into the area of faith which is essential to salvation and entrance into the Kingdom of God.

Natural and Biblical Faith; is There a Difference

Because of its importance, a clear understanding of faith as it relates to salvation is absolutely critical. Because of this, Christians use physical illustrations sometimes in an effort to help unbelievers understand faith as defined in the Bible. Although, they're done with the best of intentions, sometimes they do more harm than good. For example, consider the following illustration of faith.

A tightrope walker once placed a wire across the Grand Canyon, and then preceded to walked across that great chasm effortlessly. His climax involved the same performance while pushing a wheelbarrow. Upon completing this finality, the crowd rewarded him with accolades of praise and adulation. In response, he faced the crowd and asked for a volunteer to get in the wheelbarrow and allow him to take them to the other side. I needn't tell you the response.

To further highlight the equivalent to faith, the question is often asked, "What was the problem with the crowd"? They all had heard of this person, otherwise they would not have come to see him. Also, they witnessed his death defying stunts. Yet when asked to put their life in his hands, no one had enough confidence to do so. The problem with the crowd was a lack of trust in the tightrope walker's ability to carry a person to the other side of the chasm.

What's wrong with the illustration as it relates to biblical faith? It certainly seems to explain what it means to have faith in a person. However, the problem lies in the premise. First, even if a spectator willingly got in the wheelbarrow because of what he had seen, is that really faith; biblical or otherwise? Sure, the person's action was based on facts, assent and trust; but again is that faith? In other words, if that's all there is to it, then surely many more people would be Christians, since it points to something innate within each of us!

Regarding the issue of biblical faith, Dr. Martyn Lloyd-Jones provides this worthwhile statement, "Why, there is no difficulty about faith. We all have faith. When you sit down on a chair you are exercising faith that the chair is going to hold you . . . The argument is that we all have faith, and that all we need to do is exercise that faith that is innate in human nature, in the matter of believing God. But that is what I call applying "the law of mathematical probability". (Lloyd-Jones, D. M. *Romans: An Exposition of Chapters 3:20-4:25, Atonement ad Justification,* Grand Rapids, Michigan: Zondervan Publishing House, 1970, 232)

Dr. Lloyd-Jones bring enormous clarity to this concept of natural *faith* and biblical *faith*, and in doing so highlights the fact that what is commonly referred to as '*natural faith*' is nothing more than actions based on 'mathematical probabilities'. From the same source, Dr. Lloyd-Jones goes on to say, "When I sit on a chair I do so because I am acting on the principle that the chances are that it is not going to break down at that moment. It may at some other moment. That is the law of mathematical probability". (Lloyd-Jones, *Romans: An Exposition of Chapters 3:20-4:25*, 232)

This is why using such illustrations as sitting in a chair, or getting on an airplane; and even one as compelling as the tightrope walker to illustrate biblical faith, must be avoided; because they leave the hearer with the impression they can come to faith in Christ through their own reasoning. The reality is that Dr. Lloyd-Jones is right, what is commonly referred to as natural faith is nothing more than actions based on mathematical probabilities and therefore, no faith at all.

What is Faith

What then is biblical faith? The New Testament book of Hebrews defines it as, ". . . the substance of things hoped for, the evidence of things not seen"(Hebrews 11:1). Do you see what distinguishes biblical faith from every term used by the world? The key lies in three words; substance, hope and evidence.

First, take the word substance. In most modern translations, this word is translated as confidence. In their commentary on substance, *Jamieson, Faussett and Brown* writes, "It substantiates promises of God which we hope for, as future in fulfillment, making them present realities to us". (*JFB*, Hebrews 11:1)

This one statement in itself sets biblical faith apart and places it in a class by itself. Literally, it declares that God's promises are already confirmed and accepted by us and therefore, a present reality; even though their fulfillment is future! A good example of this is heaven! None of us has ever been there, yet we not only believe in its existence, but also everything the Bible says about it! This does not mean we understand or can fully explain it, but faith takes us beyond our natural realm into the supernatural. In doing so, it allows us to live and operate in the present in light of the realities of the future!

Faith and its Relationship to Hope

The second word or aspect of faith is hope. This is the most important word in the Christian vocabulary when it comes to living the Christian life and doing so victoriously because our life is based on hope! Actually, hope is a further explanation of the first word. What other way can God's Word be confirmed outside of hope? This is even true of hope in the physical realm. When everything else fails, hope is the one thing that keeps a person going.

Why does the unemployed person persistently looks for employment? Because of hope! Hope is the anchor that keeps and makes us go to length thought impossible, because its focus is always future. Paul sums up hope in these words, ". . . but hope that is seen is not hope: for what a man seeth, why doth he yet hope for" (Romans 8:24)?

Again, a distinction must be drawn even when we talk about hope as used in the Bible. Going back to the example of the unemployed worker. While the person can hope, his hope is based on several uncertainties, such as the economy, his skills, an employer willingness to hire him and the likes! Therefore, there always exist the potential and possibility for such hope to turn to hopelessness.

However, when it comes to biblical hope, there does not exist impossibilities because it is based on this third word, evidence; which has the idea of demonstrating or providing convincing evidence of the promises substantiated and thereby establishing the very foundation and grounds for hope!

It is true that Christians enjoy many blessings in the present, but the reality is that all God's promises lies in the future. Whether it is eternal life, spiritual rewards, glorification, or immortality; they all lie in the future and therefore, unseen to the naked eye. However, we have irrefutable evidence given to us through the word of God that such promises are true, and they are substantiated, not only to the physical mind, but first to a soul that has been changed by the Holy Spirit!

Again, let me take you back to comments from *Jamieson, Faussett and Brown* quoting John Calvin regarding those things not seen, "Eternal life is promised to us, but it is when we are dead: we are told of a blessed resurrection, but meanwhile we molder in the dust; we are declared to be justified, and sin dwells in us; we hear that we are blessed, meantime we are overwhelmed in endless miseries: we are promised abundance of all goods, but we still endure hunger and thirst; God declares He will immediately come to our help, but he seems deaf to our cries. What should we do if we had not faith and hope to lean on, and if our mind did not emerge amidst the darkness above the world by the shining of the word and Spirit of God"? (*JFB,* Hebrews 11:1)

This is the faith Paul has in mind when he declares one must, believe in him (Jesus Christ). Until a person is given the ability to exercise faith in what Jesus Christ has done for them, the new birth into the spiritual realm is not possible.

HOW IS FAITH ATTAINED

The obvious question now becomes, how is such faith possible? Paul provides the answer in the seventeenth verse of the tenth chapter of Romans, "So then faith cometh by hearing, and hearing by the word of God".

Within that verse is the second agent of the new birth, the *word of God!* Therefore, it is not just any knowledge of Jesus Christ that brings a person to the point of being born again spiritually; it is the specific knowledge of him given in the Christian Holy Bible.

I stress the source as the Christian Holy Bible to set it apart from all others, since many sects and even cults have renditions and translations of the bible and calls it the 'Holy Bible'. But only the Christian's Holy Bible sets forth clearly the redemptive work of Christ that is the foundation of the Christian faith.

Remember, confession of Jesus Christ is paramount to being saved! What are we confessing? Not only his divinity, but all he has done on our behalf, that is; being born sinless, living out the Law of God perfectly, paying the penalty of our sins by becoming sin for us and conquering death through his resurrection. Only the Christian's Holy Bible set forth these truths. This in essence is the Gospel; the good news of God (I Corinthians 15:3-4)!

This is the *word of God* preached to the world and when the Holy Spirit imparts life to the hearer, they are reborn into the spiritual realm. Why? Because they have received spiritual ears enabling them to hear the spiritual *word of God.* Within this *word* are the facts relating to the account of Jesus Christ's work on behalf of those who believe in Him.

After hearing these *words,* the Holy Spirit enables the hearer to understand the spiritual truth within them. Again, for illustration purposes only, let's return to the story of the tightrope walker? The spectators not only heard about him, they actually verified who he was by witnessing his spectacular acts. However, the fact that no one willingly got in the wheelbarrow demonstrated they did not have enough confidence in him to put their life in his hands.

The point of the illustration was to highlight, not faith, but the reality that even after hearing about Jesus Christ and the marvelous works done on our behalf, it is still not enough to give us complete faith in him. Like the tightrope walker, people probably believed he could carry any one of them across the canyon; however they lacked the necessary confidence to make them commit.

This is a crucial point! While some might conclude that any belief system is based on some form of faith, and therefore, belief is just another way of saying, "I have faith in . . .", therefore; I am now a member. That might be regarded as faith generated naturally after hearing and internalizing certain facts about the object and arriving at a specific conclusion, as in the case of the tightrope walker. But from a biblical perspective, it is not faith but is as Dr. Lloyd-Jones stressed, ". . . the law of mathematical probability". (Lloyd-Jones, *Romans: An Exposition of Chapters 3:20-4:25*, 232)

This is the reason that whenever the Bible speaks of faith, it does so from a supernatural standpoint. There's nothing natural about biblical faith, everything about it is supernatural and therefore, takes us beyond the physical realm, our intellect, and reasoning.

In conclusion, there exists this unique difference between Christianity and religions. Not only is one supernaturally born into Christianity, their choice is based upon true or biblical faith. Does this mean a person's confession of Christ as Lord and savior is not done voluntarily, as some might believe and even teach?

Though it seems that way on the surface, there's nothing further from the truth. In reality, what happens is that God imparts to the person born again by the Holy Spirit this faith as a gift (Ephesians 2:8). As such, it becomes something genuine and personal to the one born again; it becomes the individual's faith and part of their new disposition. As a result, when they hear the *good news* about Jesus Christ and all the works done on behalf of the sinner; they not only hear it clearly, they are empowered to believe its message, born again, and granted entrance into the Kingdom of God.

The purpose and intent of this chapter and the previous one was to highlight the necessity of the *Holy Spirit* and the *word of God* in Salvation.

Without both, there is no hope of ever entering the Kingdom of God. This was Jesus Christ emphasis to Nicodemus. His knowledge of the Law of God was insufficient to grant him entry into God's spiritual kingdom. He needed to be born again! That birth is only possible by the *Holy Spirit* and the *word of God.*

In summary, the sinner is called out of darkness and vanity into the kingdom of God by the *Holy Spirit's* power and the *word of God.* This process is called the new birth. This was the essence of Jesus' words to Nicodemus that, "Ye must be born of the Spirit and water"!

QUESTIONS TO PONDER:

1. Why is it dangerous to have a new believer repeat the sinner's prayer?
2. John 1:12 is often used as an evangelistic tool. How has this chapter help you better understand this verse and its relationship to regeneration?
3. Discuss the relationship between the Holy Spirit, God's Word and faith in a person's salvation. Are all three needed? Is the order, i.e. can one be saved by hearing the word first apart from receiving the Holy Spirit? Explain your answers.
4. The illustration of the tightrope walker is often used to illustrate the meaning of faith. How has this chapter help you better understand the importance of exercising caution when using physical illustrations to explain spiritual truths?

CHAPTER 12

Justification

Simul iustus et peccator! This famous Latin phrase spoken by Martin Luther, of the Protestant reformation means *"at the same time sinner and saint"*. Though on the surface, it seems contradictory, it is the best and easiest way of explaining the end result of *justification*. Basically it means that the person who confess the Lord Jesus Christ as Lord and Savior remains a sinner because the sin nature still reside in them. However, at the same time, they are declared righteous by God! How can this be? In other words, how can a person be both sinner and Christian at the same time? This lies at the heart of *justification* and is the focus of this chapter

WHAT IS JUSTIFICATION

Many Christians believe their salvation was the direct result of their ability to see their spiritual deficiency and reach out to Jesus Christ for deliverance. God, through His omniscience, seeing this desire in turn elects and eventually calls them to salvation. Perhaps this mind-frame is a key factor in the belief that a person's salvation is never secure. After all, if my works saved me, then logically, works are required to maintain and keep that salvation.

However, the one question never asked by such Christians is, "By whom, or by what standard are my works being judged"? This is a critical question because if the standard is unknown or unclear, how does one know when they have been met or satisfied? This is the problem with world religions, there is never any guarantee that the worshipper has met and satisfied their 'god's' requirements.

This is not the case with Christianity because God removes all uncertainty by clearly setting forth, not many, but his single standard for pleasing him; a life lived in perfect righteousness, both internally and externally. This is the only standard acceptable to God and is the only one by which all will be judged! Perfect righteousness by a perfect judge!

Unfortunately, when God's standard is laid beside each individual's life, we clearly see the depth of our sin and corruption. As a result of our lack of goodness, or righteousness, God declares all humanity guilty, condemned and under the penalty of death (Romans 3:10)! While some might object, His judgment is just and righteous because it is based on the fact that man's every thought, every deed, and every intention is imperfect and evil because they originate from the sin force. Since this is the condition of all humanity, how can anyone ever expect to meet so high, and in reality, impossible standard? This is the question answered by *justification.*

Having said that, the obvious question becomes; what is *justification?* First, it is *forensic,* or *legal,* in nature. In the context of our discussion, the term *forensic* has to do with the legal declaration made by God regarding the status, or as indicated earlier, the position of the sinner and their relationship to God's law. In order to understand its significance and relationship to *justification,* the reader is reminded of the earlier chapters on Adam's sin; its impact on him, and all humanity. When he sinned, he violated God's law; and as a righteous judge, the lawgiver legally declared him guilty and at the same time sentenced him to the penalty of death! Not only was he legally declared guilty, his guilt and penalty was passed onto us (Romans 5:12). This described the spiritual state, or condition, of Adam and his posterity! There is only one remedy to both Adam and humanity's condition; the judge must have a change of heart, or he must acquit the violator. Since God is immutable, or changeless, the former is not possible; therefore, the only alternative for humanity is the judge's acquittal.

That is the crux of *justification;* God the righteous judge acquits the sinner. This is why it is *forensic* in nature; it deals with the issue of God's law and man's violation of that law. But not even God can acquit the unrighteous, His justice will not allow it. And even though the term means to declare righteous, such a declaration is not done without the penalty incurred by the violator being satisfied. In the ensuing sections of this chapter, we will look at the various aspects of this wonderful doctrine.

Two Aspects of Justification: An Alien Righteousness and Imputation

Having defined the nature of *justification,* this leads to the second aspect; *justification* has no internal effect on the person being justified. As stated earlier, it is a declaration made by God affecting the sinner's status or position. Unlike regeneration, *justification* is not something that happens within the Christian, its affect and actions are external and spiritual. Martin Luther described it best by another one of his famous phrases, it is an, *"alien righteousness"*.

In explaining this phrase, Dr. R. C. Sproul writes, "This is the righteousness of another, one who is a 'foreigner' to us, not in the sense that he is unknown by us or that he remains a mysterious stranger to us, but in the sense that he is ever and always distinguishable from us, even though by faith we are 'in' him and he is 'in' us"[4]. This is another reason why no one can boast of having any part in their salvation because every Christian is saved, not by their merit, but by the merits of another; namely Jesus Christ!

This naturally leads to a third aspect of *justification,* the doctrine of *imputation.* Since the righteousness that saves us is foreign, the obvious question becomes, how does it become ours? The answer lies in what is called, *imputation*! The statement was made earlier that God's standard for saving anyone is perfect righteousness, or 'sinlessness'; and there lies the problem with all people. As stated earlier, Adam could only produce beings in his own corrupt and sinful likeness and image (Genesis 5:3). Therefore, the greatest and purest person (by man's standard) with all their good deeds, stand imperfect and condemned before God because of their intimate relationship with Adam and his sin nature (Romans 5:12)!

That's the significance of *imputation.* The term itself comes from the world of accounting and deals with account ledgers. The best way to understand it is to imagine a ledger detailing a person's accrued debt for a certain period of time. For the sake of argument, let's assume this person has accumulated a debt of one trillion dollars and has only one week to pay it back. When compound interest is added to this scenario, it becomes

---

4   Sproul, R. C. *Faith Alone, The Evangelical Doctrine of Justification.* Grand Rapids, Michigan: Baker Books, 1995

obvious that the person in question would find themselves in a hopeless and impossible situation.

Now bring to this person's situation the ledger of the richest man in the world who agrees to not simply take that person's debt, but transfer all his wealth to the ledger of that hopeless person. The debt has been paid, not with the debtor's money but that of another. This is a crude but adequate illustration of *imputation*. It sets before us the picture of the imperfect sinner owing a debt of righteousness that he or she is unable to pay, no matter how many good deeds they're done, or regardless of how many sacraments attended—they all fall short of God's standard (Romans 3:20).

It is easy to see how this simple illustration helps our understanding of *imputation*. The sinner has acquired a debt and a penalty he is unable to repay; red ink fills his ledger so completely, there is no room left for one single drop of red ink! This is the state of all mankind and if they are to clear their ledger of their accrued debt, they need the riches of another.

In *imputation* then, God legally transfers the infinite righteousness from the ledger of His Son Jesus Christ to the sinner's ledger of debt (sins). At the same time, God transfers the sinner's debt to the ledger of His Son Jesus Christ. Now, Jesus Christ's righteousness is accounted to the sinner's account and the sinner's sin is accounted to Jesus Christ. It is a double action and is sometimes referred to as *'double imputation'* (Illustration 1).

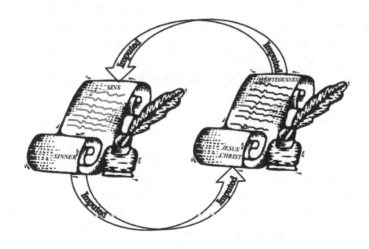

Double imputation

In the process of *imputation,* God remains the *just* God and can now legally declare the sinner guiltless, not because of who he is inherently, but because of this *'alien'* righteousness that has been accounted to him. Though the sinner still remains unchanged internally, his relationship to the sin force has been totally changed in this way. First, According to Romans 5:1, there is peace with God. The sin force's power has been defeated and the sinner is now reunited with God.

Second, Romans 5:1 further states, we can experience God's love in our innermost being. What joy comes to the heart of the one justified, to be able to experience the blessings and joys of being reunited with the Creator!

There is a third benefit of being *justified,* adoption into the family of God (Romans 8:15:16)! And because we have been adopted into the family of God, the Apostle Paul reminds us that we are joint-heirs with Jesus Christ (Romans 8:17).

But the greatest benefit of *justification* is found in Romans 8:1; "There is therefore now no condemnation to them which are in Christ Jesus". This blessing, made possible by and through *imputation* is the Christian's greatest joy! Before, all of humanity was under God's judgment, wrath and condemnation. But once confession of faith is made in Jesus Christ, our whole status and position changes; we become part of God's family!

This is the glory of *imputation,* the manifestation of God's immeasurable love in that He *imputes* his son's righteousness to our account; thus making Him sin for us (2 Corinthians 5:21). This is grace, this is mercy and this is *imputation*! Without this, God could no more save the sinner than a just judge could legally allow a convicted criminal to go free!

ASPECTS OF JUSTIFICATION: PROPITIATION

The third aspect of *justification* is *propitiation*. This term is not one commonly talked or preached about today. It has to do with God's *justice* being satisfied and is closely linked to *imputation*. Earlier, the point was made that *justification* is a forensic act whereby God declares the sinner acquitted! However, what was omitted at that time was the fact that, that acquittal is not possible apart from God's justice being satisfied first! The Bible refers to this 'satisfaction of God's justice' as *propitiation*.

One must never think or believe that God winks at sin and unrighteousness; nor should any person imagine or believe that in the end

God will grant both sinner and agnostic, or even, atheist and blasphemer eternal life and a mansion in heaven. Paul makes this fact clear in his words to the philosophers at Mars Hill in Acts 17:30. Listen to his words, "And the times of this ignorance God winked at; but now commandeth all men every where to repent". The time of ignorance referred to by Paul is the time prior to the revelation of the Gospel of Jesus Christ. During that time in history God '*winked*' at man's ignorance. In some translations, the word '*winked*' is translated '*overlooked*'.

Unfortunately, too many Christians forget this fact, the language of Scripture must be interpreted in light of the culture from which it was written. For this reason many wrongly interpret the word '*overlooked*' as meaning God condones sin. But nothing could be further from the truth. Notice John Gill's explanation regarding the usage of this word, ". . . he despised this, and them for it, and was displeased and angry with them; and as an evidence of such contempt and indignation, he overlooked them, and took no notice of them, and gave them no revelation to direct them, nor prophets to instruct them, and left them to their stupidity and ignorance". (John Gill, *John Gill's Exposition*, Acts 17:30)

Based on Gill's comments, we conclude this from Paul's argument in Acts 17:30; there was a time when God left humanity to itself, allowing them to live according to their own devices. However, Paul provides a strong contrast in the latter part of Acts 17:30 by comparing God's actions towards humanity in the past to that of the present. In other words, in the past, God '*took no notice*' of humanity and "gave them no revelation to direct them, nor prophets to instruct them'. As a result, they were left to 'their stupidity and ignorance".

But now a radical change has occurred, God has sent his son to resolve the one issue that separated himself from humanity—sin! God took notice of humanity's pitiful and hopeless plight and not only sent his only begotten son to suffer and die on our behalf, but revealed this reality to us through the preaching of the Gospel.

The revelation and preaching of the Gospel ushers in a new period, a new era and a new responsibility. Humanity is no longer ignorant of their sin, nor are they ignorant of God's provision to deal with them. Therefore, Paul declares that God now commands all men and women everywhere to repent! There are no exceptions, all must repent to escape God's judgment (Acts 17:31)! Repentance means a change of direction, a change of mind, or a change in one's thinking.

Think of Paul's audience in the seventeenth chapter of Acts. These men lived for themselves and had no idea God had already judged and sentenced them to death because of Adam's sin. Their only hope of acquittal from this penalty was to have the debt incurred by them through Adam satisfied! Until that's done, they remain in their sin and therefore, guilty, condemned and on their way to eternal damnation and ultimately the lake-of-fire!!

That's the principle behind *justification* and the essence of the Gospel—humanity's debt has been paid through the life and death of Jesus Christ! On that basis, and that basis alone, God now declares the sinner *just* or *justified* because he has been *propitiated;* his *justice* has been satisfied.

This is the truth that often goes unnoticed during Good Friday's celebrations all over the country—the satisfaction of God's *justice* at Calvary; he was *propitiated!* All humanity stand guilty, condemned and under God's wrath, that's the legal penalty passed upon all because of Adam's disobedience. This means that everyone who has not confessed their faith in the work of Jesus Christ on the cross will stand before God; the supreme judge, to answer for their violation of his Law.

That's why what happened on Calvary's cross must never be forgotten. Perhaps this was in the mind of the great hymn writer Isaac Watts when he penned these wonderful words in the song, *At the Cross,*

> But drops of grief can ne'er repay the debt of love I owe;
> Here, Lord, I give myself away; tis all that I can do.

What can we offer to a God who has done all that is necessary to satisfy his own *justice?* Not only did he give his Only Begotten Son, he made him sin for us! That's why during his crucifixion, Jesus cried, "My God, my God, why hast thou forsaken me", (Matthew 27:46)? As the sin-bearer, he bore the totality of all the sins committed by those elected by God.

Think about this for a moment, how many sins will one person commit in their lifetime in deed and thought? One thousand or a thousand times a thousand? The reality is, whatever that number is, multiply it by all the other sins of every one of God's elect (both alive and dead) and what you have is a mass of sin unimaginable to any one of us. The Bible says that God took those accumulated sins and put them on his Son making him sin (2 Corinthians 5:21). It was for that reason he, God the father, had to separate himself, or forsake his Son on that dark Friday! Stop here for a second and ponder this truth. Stop here and meditate on the wonder and immeasurable depth of God's love for those whom he elected; despite the fact they were vessels fitted for destruction!

THE SATISFACTION OF GOD'S JUSTICE DEMONSTRATED IN THE OLD TESTAMENT

Few other doctrines of our faith highlight the importance of a proper understanding of the Old Testament sacrificial system than *propitiation*, especially in the yearly ceremony performed by the Jewish High Priest on the Day of Atonement. On that day, the High Priest, took two male goats from the congregation of Israel as an offering for sin (Leviticus 16:5, GW).

One goat was set apart and slain as a sin offering or sacrifice to the LORD for all the people of Israel (Leviticus 16:8, 9). His blood was then taken by the High Priest into the Holy of Holies, the innermost compartment of the Tabernacle where it was sprinkled on a golden lid covering the Ark of the Covenant called the Mercy Seat.

Seen here in this one act is a wonderful picture of God's mercy. Within the Ark of the Covenant were the two tablets containing the Ten Commandments. Can you see the shadow of *justice* being met with mercy? The nation as a whole had broken God's Law and by all rights, they deserved death! However, instead of dispensing *justice*, God passes that penalty upon another who stood in their stead. When the blood of the substitute was sprinkled on the Mercy Seat, the penalty of the people's sin had been met (albeit symbolically), and God's justice was satisfied, or *propitiated*.

Before proceeding and for clarity sake, it does need to be reemphasize, all this was symbolic and not actual. They were what are called *types* or *shadows*. That is, in and of themselves, they had no effectual benefit to the one on whose behalf they were done or given (Hebrews 10:4, 8). They could only portray or point to the reality of a specific truth not yet fully revealed.

The Significance of the Sacrifice

Additionally, the actions of the High Priest highlight two things about the people. First, it showed their inability to atone or pay the penalty for their own sins. They needed a substitute, something or someone who was regarded as perfect in the eyes of God and who could stand in their stead. In this case, it was the goat.

Clarity at this point is important lest anyone should believe the blood of goats or sheep was sufficient in and of themselves to satisfy God's *justice* (Hebrews 10:4). The Hebrew writer makes it plain that God took no pleasure in such sacrifices precisely because they had no redeeming merit (Hebrews 10:4, 6, 8). It pleased God to have the people do so as a symbol or picture of how he would eventually solve the sin issue. When the writer of the New Testament letter of Hebrews declares that God took no pleasure in these sacrifices, its importance to understand this is what he meant by that statement.

He does not mean the acts themselves displeased God, otherwise they would have been without purpose and therefore, utterly futile. God's displeasure was not in the act itself but in the reality that at stake was not the redemption or satisfaction of an animal's violation; but that of human beings. Therefore, it did not matter how many animals the people slayed; they could never atone or *propitiate* God's *justice* for humans. That aspect of the process displeased God, but it was necessary in order to give us the picture of redemption and help us fully understand the purpose and reason for Christ dying on the cross!

Second, it sets before us the very reason *imputation* is necessary. Neither the High Priest nor any other person could die in the place of the nation since they were all sinners and imperfect, just as are all men and women today. Again, not only because of our own sins, but because we all were seminally present in Adam at the time he sinned.

There is nothing profound about this statement as it is the principle that like begets like. No one plants a fig tree and expects an apple tree to spring forth because it defies the laws of nature. Likewise, Adam could not produce any other kind of being except one like himself, a sinner (Genesis 5:3). So in essence, no one, including Adam, is perfect enough to die for the sins of another human.

The other part of the events performed on the Day of Atonement involved the second goat or the *scapegoat*, which was not slain. Instead,

God commanded the High Priest to, "place both hands on its head. He will confess over it all the sins, all the rebellious acts, and all the things the Israelites did wrong. He will transfer them to the goat's head" (Leviticus 16:21, GW). Again, in this act is the shadow or illustration of *imputation.*

Not only is this goat not slain, he is led away from the camp along with the sins of the people symbolically transferred from them to him, into the wilderness. Why was he taken away from the camp? The camp, you remember, was where the Tabernacle and the glory of God was. Therefore, leading the goat away (with the people's sin), from the camp symbolized the people's sins being sent away from God's presence. In doing so, the relationship between God and his people Israel, severed by sin, is now restored. This act is referred to as *expiation* meaning to *send away.* Another and perhaps more common term is *remission* of sins.

THE PURPOSES OF SHADOWS OR TYPES IN THE OLD TESTAMENT

As stated earlier, these were shadows or types which pointed to the ultimate means of how God would eventually *justify* his people. By looking at the pictures we see clearly what Christ has done for us and why God can declare those who express faith in Jesus Christ *just* or righteous! Just as the High Priest chose those two goats to fulfill God's total requirement for the penalty of sin, so did our high priest Jesus Christ become the reality of the things that could only be symbolized by the goats. How did he do this?

First, in the account of the High Priest duties on the Day of Atonement, we find that he himself was just as guilty as those on whom behalf he was acting and therefore, a sacrifice had to be presented to God on behalf of himself and his family's sin (Leviticus 16:6). Only then was he in a position to perform the high priestly duties on behalf of the people.

Second, there had to be both satisfaction or a *propitiation* and *expiation* for our sins, that's the reason for the two goats. One had to die while the other had to bear and remove the people's sin from the presence of God.

In Christ we have the High Priest, who himself had no sin and therefore had no need for a sacrifice. Because He is fully God and fully human, he not only offered himself as the perfect and infinite sacrifice, he also took our sins upon himself. Paul declares in his second letter to the church at Corinth that, God made him sin (2 Corinthians 5:21).

However, having said all that, one thing must be made clear; in making this statement about Christ becoming sin, the Apostle Paul is not alluding to, nor is he implying that Jesus had a sin nature (John 8:46; Hebrews 7:26; I Peter 2:22; I John 3:5)! If that were the case, his sacrifice was just as worthless as the two thieves beside Him.

This is the significance of understanding the purpose and role of the scape goat. When the High Priest placed his hand on the goats head, there was no literal transfer of sin, and even if it was, it could do nothing for our salvation because he was an animal. The fact of the matter is that an animal could never atone for the sins of a human, because they had not sinned, man had! Therefore, atonement had to be done by a man.

The physical picture presented of the goats highlighted the fact that the sins of the people were not infused into the *scapegoat* by the actions of the High Priest. They were symbolically transferred or laid upon him. This is the same idea behind Paul's statement in the passage from 2 Corinthians 5:21. The difference is that in the case of Christ, God actually laid upon him the actual *sins* of those elected to be saved. Therefore, when Jesus Christ was crucified, he literally took upon himself our sins!

But that's not all! The Jews insisted that the Romans crucify Jesus outside the walls of Jerusalem. Their request was based on the fact that the Jewish Temple was located inside the walls of Jerusalem. Though the glory of God had long since left the Temple and therefore, its religious significance was all but lost, the Jewish religious leaders still maintained its sacredness.

Ironically, their insistence on this act fulfilled the role of the *scapegoat.*

Earlier in this book, the statement was made that election is the core of the church. If that statement is true, then *justification* must be the church's very foundation for without it, all the other doctrines of the Christian faith are meaningless. In other words, none could be executed until God's *justice* had been satisfied! Dr. R.C. Sproul writes this quote from Martin Luther in his book *Faith Alone* regarding the significance of *justification,* "The article of Justification is the master and prince, the lord, the ruler, and the judge over all kinds of doctrines; it preserves and governs all church doctrine and raises up our conscience before God. Without this article the world is utter death and darkness".[5] Luther's statement says it all, without *justification,* "the world would be utter death and darkness", indeed!

QUESTIONS TO PONDER:

1. Why must we be justified?
2. How do you explain Luther's statement that we are sinner and saint at the same time?
3. If God took no pleasure in the sacrifices done in the Old Testament, why did he command the people to perform them?
4. What is the importance of imputation and propitiation?
5. How is propitiation different from expiation? Why are both necessary?
6. What truths were symbolized during the ceremonies performed on the Day of Atonement?

---

5   Sproul, R. C. *Faith Alone, The Evangelical Doctrine of Justification.* Grand Rapids, Michigan: Baker Books, 1995

CHAPTER 13

Sanctification

In the twelfth chapter of the New Testament book of Romans, Paul opens up with these words, "I beseech you therefore, brethren, by the mercies of God, that ye present your bodies a living sacrifice, holy, acceptable unto God, which is your reasonable service".

The word that grabs our attention in that verse is present. This term is the same one used in the Old Testament of the worshipper's act of presenting their sacrifice to the priest on the Day of Atonement. This act perfectly illustrates the sinner's inability to approach or atone for their sins by or through their own merit. Because of their sin, they could only present a substitute to God on their behalf.

However, as discussed in the previous chapter, all this changed after Jesus Christ's became our substitute and died on the cross. Because of his redemptive work, those exercising faith in Him are justified or made right with God. Therefore, 'being justified', we are no longer sinners but are in a position to offer ourselves to God. Paul says this act is the Christian's reasonable service.

The Greek word translated 'reasonable' in this verse means 'rational'. The first eleven chapters of Romans are Paul's discourse on salvation. From chapters one through the first twenty verses of chapter three, he sets forth man's sinful condition and the awful manifestation of that condition. Having done that, he then sets before us in verse twenty-one of chapter three to the end of chapter four, all that God did to redeem the elect. Chapters five and eight (chapters six and seven being parenthetical) highlight the benefits gained by those who are justified through faith in Jesus Christ. Finally, in chapters nine to the end of chapter eleven, Paul details the relationship between salvation and God's ultimate plan for the Jews.

After reading and understanding the content of all that is written in the first eleven chapters of Romans, Paul concludes that a person's reasonable or rational response is to willingly present themselves to God in worship. Again, there is nothing radical about this statement! Imagine a beggar, blind and destitute; in essence, one void of any means of support. Now, imagine a millionaire out of pity for this poor, wretched soul, taking him to his home and not only cleaning him up, but making him one of his children and joint-heir to his inheritance!

What would his reaction be towards his benefactor? Would he not give his whole self to him as a sign of gratitude? Well something much grander and eternal has happened to the Christian. That is the idea behind Paul's words in the first verse of the twelfth chapter of Romans; and this whole idea of presenting ourselves to God is encapsulated in the doctrine of *sanctification*.

WHAT IS SANCTIFICATION

Put in its simplest form, *sanctification* is the 'outliving' or 'outworking' of God's Word through the power of the Holy Spirit in the life of the Christian among those that we live, work and associate. It is the essence of being salt and light in the world.

This is an important truth because there is so much confusion surrounding this particular doctrine. One is the teaching that sanctification means living a life totally free from sin. Because of the absurdity of such teachings, there should not be a need to devote any attention to it. However, we live in a time where Satan's ministers have crept into the church and wrecked lives, shaken some Christian's faith; and compromised the integrity and character of the church through false teaching! One of the areas where this is evident is in the teaching on *sanctification*. Having said that, let us briefly examine some truths about this critical doctrine of the Christian faith.

The first truth about *sanctification* deserving our attention is to understand its relationship to *justification*. When talking about salvation, these two processes and teachings must never be separated. To be clear, I do not mean we should see them as being synonymous, because they're not. My point is that we should see them as two sides of the same coin. In other words, a person who is *justified* is a person where *sanctification* has already begun. In other words, *justification* is external whereas *sanctification* is an inward work done inside the Christian. If all Christians knew and understood this particular fact about *sanctification*, the belief that one could lose their salvation would not be as extensive as it is in Christendom.

Second, since *sanctification* is a process begun by the Holy Spirit, it means that it is more than an experience; it is a process that begins where *justification* leaves of. Again, I hesitate to speak in this fashion for fear that it might evoke in the readers' mind a sense of phases. In other words, phase one is regeneration, phase two is faith and so forth. This is not the position that I am trying to convey or promote. Instead, my goal is to try and help Christians understand there are individual acts involved in salvation, and an understanding of those acts helps us better understand how and why we are saved. So when I talk about the connection between *justification* and *sanctification*, the focus is not on the phase, but the fact that you cannot have one without the other.

Third, though *sanctification* is begun by the Holy Spirit, it is not a process where the Christian is passive. This is what sets it apart from *justification*. As discussed in the previous chapter, God acts upon us in *justification*. However, in *sanctification*, God acts in us through the Holy Spirit and his word. Here, is where the Christian cease being passive because now he or she must not only avail themselves of God's Word through study and meditation, but partner with the Holy Spirit in order to make that word an active part of their very being.

That was the point behind the statement in the earlier section of this chapter which highlighted the role of the Holy Spirit and God's Word in *sanctification*. A proper understanding of this basic fact avoids the misinterpretation of *sanctification* being regarded merely as an experience, or that it is experiential only.

Admittedly, it sounds spiritual and even biblically correct and reasonable! However, *sanctification* has to be more than that! Without argument, experience is needed, but that experience is not *sanctification*. The only reason so many Christians believe this to be the case is due to a lack of teaching in this area.

Therefore, to understand this crucial doctrine and its relationship to our experiences, it's best to examine it from God's perspective. First, all humanity is either in a position of condemnation and under God's wrath; or saved and under his grace. This must be clear in every person's mind, there is no middle ground! Furthermore, this standing is based on a person's relationship to God.

As stated earlier, *justification* satisfies God's righteous requirement, declaring those who trust in Jesus Christ as Savior, righteous before him. This change is relational and places the person in a position where he or she is no longer condemned and under God's wrath. Instead, Scripture calls such a person a *saint*. Again, this is a spiritual process, involving God the Father and the regenerated person's exercising faith in the finished work of Jesus Christ done on their behalf.

Understanding the Relationship Between Sanctification, and Justification

The term *saint* is new to our discussion, yet significant to a proper understanding of *sanctification*. This term comes from the same root word as holy, one of God's attributes. It is his holiness that separates him from humanity because of its sinfulness. In other words (and as stressed throughout this book) it is man's sin that separates him from God! The only possible solution to this problem is to either eradicate sin from the individual or have someone take on the creature's sin.

Since the former is impossible, God in his grace and mercy sent his only Begotten Son into the world to not only fulfill the Law for us, but also made him to be sin for the elect (2 Corinthians 5:21). The purpose behind it all was so that, "we might be made the righteousness of God in him". This is another way of saying we are *justified* in Christ. Our position and relationship to God has been changed; not because of our inherent righteousness, but because of Christ's own imputed righteousness to us!

The point in saying all this is to repeat the principle, that *justification* not only changes our position and relationship to God, it sets us apart, or makes us different from those not saved. Again, not physically different, we're still human beings, still imperfect and still indwelt by the sin nature. But because God declares us righteous, we are essentially not in the same condition, or state, as we were before being *justified*.

Paul gives a beautiful contrast between these two lifestyles in 1 Corinthians 6: 9 11. Notice what he says,

> "[9] Know ye not that the unrighteous shall not inherit the kingdom of God? Be not deceived: neither fornicators,

nor idolaters, nor adulterers, nor effeminate, nor abusers of themselves with mankind, [10] Nor thieves, nor covetous, nor drunkards, nor revilers, nor extortioners, shall inherit the kingdom of God. [11] And such were some of you: but ye are washed, but ye are sanctified, but ye are justified in the name of the Lord Jesus, and by the Spirit of our God.

Do you see the contrast? In verse nine and ten, Paul describes the life of the unsaved as one lived entirely apart from the righteousness of God. However, in verse 11, Paul reminds the Corinthians, this was also their former way of life. This was their position or condition, not necessarily by man's standards, but God's.

Paul continues in verse eleven by further stating that, that's who they were before coming to Christ, but now they were "washed, sanctified and justified in the name of the Lord Jesus Christ, and by the Spirit of God".

The behavior of the Christians in Corinth was horrific, so much so that it prompted a stern rebuke from Paul in the fifth chapter of that same letter. Their behavior did not conform to their position. They were *saints* (I Corinthians 1:2), yet they were acting like sinners (1 Corinthians 3:1, 3).

Therefore, Paul has to remind them that they were washed. Unfortunately, the King James Version does not give the full impact of Paul's actual words. What he actually said was, "Ye have had yourselves washed". No longer were their hearts filled with the stain and filth of sin, it had already been thoroughly washed by the blood of Jesus Christ through the Holy Spirit. This one-time act occurred at regeneration. Had they forgotten or not realized this? Certainly their actions seem to indicate they had.

Not only had they been washed, they were *sanctified.* Since this term has in view the work of Jesus Christ and the Holy Spirit, it has to mean more than just being set apart unto God. Paul wants to emphasize the internal operation done by the Spirit at regeneration on the sinner's hearts; changing its disposition from one of hostility towards God to one longing to do the things which pleases him. This new disposition infused into the soul at regeneration now begets a new principle where pleasing and doing the will of God is supreme.

Finally, Paul tells the Corinthian Christians they are *justified.* The order given in this verse has caused some confusion because it puts *justification* last. The biblical view of salvation is justification, washing, and sanctification. The reason Paul reverses the order in this instance sprang from the immediate problem facing the Corinthians; their problem was one of practice, not conversion. In other words, he's teaching those already saved about the inconsistency of that reality with their current practice. In order to make clear his point, he reminds them of the inner work already done by the Spirit of God.

By reversing the order, he keeps the focus on the matter at hand, mainly their ungodly behavior, on the one hand, and the work of the Spirit on the other. His concern at this point is not *justification* in its legal or forensic sense, but the Spirit's role in that process. Regarding I Corinthians 6:11, John Gill states that *justification*, ". . . here, is to be understood of their being justified in the court of conscience, under the witnessing of the Spirit of God". Gill continues by highlighting the Holy Spirit's specific work after regeneration of, "having convinced them of the insufficiency of their own righteousness, and having brought near the righteousness of Christ unto them, and wrought faith in them to lay hold on it, pronounced them justified persons in their own consciences". (John Gill, *John Gill's Exposition,* I Corinthians 6:11)

Paul's statement to the Christians at Corinth emphasize the fundamental principle behind *sanctification* and why it should not be seen first, as an experience. Instead, it is the outworking of the Holy Spirit in our lives as we surrender our members to him.

SANCTIFICATION IS PROGRESSIVE

Positionally, the person confessing Jesus Christ as Lord is already *sanctified*, or set apart; that occurred during *justification* and can never change! A holy seed was implanted within them by the Spirit of God. However, like a seed planted by a farmer, it needs other elements if it is to grow. The Corinthians were like many Christians today, who believe *sanctification* is a completed act at conversion. This is true of positional *sanctification* only! Now the Christian must become actively involved with the Holy Spirit in outliving that which is true of them from a positional standpoint. This is commonly referred to as *progressive sanctification* (see image on next page).

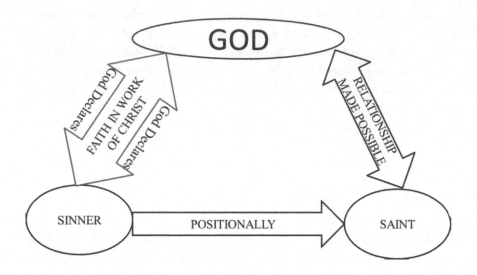

The relationship Between Justification and Sanctification

Some denominations deny the progressive nature of *sanctification* and instead teach that it is complete at some point in a Christian's life; usually symbolized by speaking in tongues, or some other ecstatic experience. However, nothing is further from the truth! Sanctification is an ongoing process that begins when a person is converted and does not end until the point of glorification. In other words, in this life, it is humanly impossible to perfectly live out God's requirements because we still have the sin force residing in our nature.

While it has no power over us, there are times when we will sin! However, when we do, it does not mean that we do not know God's love for us; nor does it mean that we are not still filled with all the fullness of God's spirit. Instead, it demonstrates we are not yet perfect and comprise experiences that further *sanctification* (Galatians 5:17). It is our understanding of all God has done for and to us along with our daily experiences that progressively move us closer and closer to being conformed to the image of Jesus Christ. While the completion of that work will not happen until the day we're glorified; as Christians, we press on through the difficulties and trials faced on a daily basis: this is *progressive sanctification* and is experiential! As we grow in the knowledge of God's Word, we are made stronger through the Holy Spirit. The Christian who neglect God's Word has no anchor and impedes sanctification!

Regarding our experiences and the need to know doctrine, Dr. Lloyd-Jones writes, "The doctrines and experiences provide us with the motive of sanctification. They are intended and designed to create a desire within us for sanctification. They are designed to show us the possibility of sanctification by reminding us of the power that works in us in order that we may work it out". (Lloyd-Jones, D. M. *Christian Unity, An Exposition of Ephesians 4:1-16.* Grand Rapids: Baker Book House, 1980, 18)

This is Paul's reason for talking to the Christians at Corinth as he did. They had lost all motivation to live holy because they either had forgotten who they were in Christ or where God had brought them. This still holds true today. Christians live defeated lives spiritually, not because they are not *sanctified,* but because they lack the two necessary elements to motivate them to live a holy life; mainly doctrine and experiences.

If the farmer plants a seed in the ground, it will not grow if deprived the of rain and sunshine. Likewise, a regenerated soul deprived of the word of God will not lead to experiences because it has nothing to anchor it (I Corinthians 10:13). On the other hand, the soul that is filled with God's Word will experience the joy and peace of God when trials and temptation confronts him or her in life (Romans 5:1-5). As they overcome them, they not only grow closer to God, but become more like Christ. This is *sanctification!*

QUESTIONS TO PONDER:

1. Is it possible to be justified and not sanctified? Explain.
2. Explain why it is proper to regard all Christians as saints.
3. Is it wrong to regard some Christians as being more sanctified than others? Explain.
4. What does the term progressive sanctification mean?

CHAPTER 14

Glorification

What is the end of our salvation, that is, to what purpose has God saved us? This has to be a crucial question or at least a concern to anyone who is saved. If our salvation is simply an act done to us by God, just to give us a better life here on earth with no eternal benefits, then we are no better-off than those comprising the various religious sects of the day.

But thank God, this is not the case! In the eighth chapter of the book of Romans, the Spirit of God gives us the answer to God's purpose for saving us; it is, "to conform us to the image of his beloved Son"!

GLORIFICATION AND BEING CONFORMED

What does the Bible mean when it talks about *glorification* and how does the word *'conform'* help in our understanding. First, let us examine this word *'conform'*. In the Greek, it is a compound word meaning, 'to bring to the same form with'. All of us are familiar with this idea from our experiences in life. Take, for example, the name, chili con carne. Regardless of its use, the common understanding by everyone is that we're talking about chili with meat; coming from the word 'con' meaning together with; and 'carne' for flesh or meat.

This same idea is in mind when Paul used this word in Romans chapter eight. The exception, off course, to our example is the word 'form' which literally means to 'be like someone else in form, to bring into the same form as someone else'. (Lloyd-Jones, D. M. *Romans: An Exposition of Chapter 8:17-39: The Final Perseverence of the Saints*. Edinburgh, Scotland: The Banner of Truth Trust, 1998, 223) Perhaps an example would be useful here. During the Chicago Bulls reign as the National Basketball Champion, the common phrase 'to be like Mike' emerged.

The essence of this phrase evolved around Michael Jordan's phenomenon athletic ability. There was no one with his jumping and scoring ability like 'his airness'. All this was manifested in his *form*! His was one uniquely his own and therefore, set him apart from all other basketball players of his time!

But in reality, to be like Mike meant that a person would have to have all those traits and abilities that made Michael Jordan who he is innately. The problem, however, lies in the reality that those qualities were innate and therefore, part of his being and individuality. Therefore, to have his form means one would have to share or become an integral part of him, something quite impossible!

This simple human example helps us understand Paul's use of the word when referring to Christians becoming *conformed* to the image of Jesus Christ. When we look at ourselves, we do not look much like him, neither in deed or character. But all Christians are on their way to being shaped and molded or *conformed* into his image.

This is the work of the Holy Spirit in sanctification. While this work (ultimate sanctification), will never be achieved in our mortal body, it is God's ultimate objective for the elect! The Spirit of God assures us of this reality through the Apostle John with these words, "Beloved, now are we the sons of God, and it doth not yet appear what we shall be: but we know that, when he shall appear, we shall be like him; for we shall see him as he is" (I John 3:2)! He (the Spirit), further declares through the Apostle Paul that this complete conformation; where God *conforms* us to the image of his son, happens, "In the twinkling of an eye", (I Corinthians 15:52a)!

But there is a second word in the phrase; "to be conformed into the image of his Son", deserving of our immediate attention, and that is the word *image*. In his commentary on this verse, Dr. Martyn Lloyd-Jones states, "Image means more than a 'likeness'; it is a special type of likeness. It is not an accidental likeness, but a 'derived likeness'. In this statement, Dr. Lloyd-Jones draws a distinction between something that looks like something or someone else because of what it is in contrast to a derived likeness. He further writes, "We sometimes say of a child, 'He is the exact image of his father'. If that is so, it is because he has derived the likeness from his father". (Lloyd-Jones, *Romans: An Exposition of Chapter 8:17-39*, 223)

God wants Christians to be able to grasp the reality that the work he began in our lives at the point of our salvation is one that culminates in our being conformed to the image of Jesus Christ (Philippians 1:6). We will be like him; in form and in a likeness derived from him!

This is the reason the Apostle Paul declares, "we shall be like him" (I John 3:2b)! This is the basis for examining the two terms; *conformed* and *image*. Both help us understand that the ultimate goal of salvation is *glorification,* and glorification is not possible apart from our bodies being conformed to the image of Jesus Christ!

Having looked at the necessity of being conformed to Jesus Christ's image, the obvious question on the minds of most is, ". . . with what body are we resurrected and glorified" (I Corinthians 15:35, my emphasis)? At some point, this topic is bound to come up when talking about *glorification,* even if the person is unsaved.

THE NATURE OF THE GLORIFIED BODY

"What kind of body will this conformation bring about"? Like the example involving Michael Jordan; setting a goal to become like him is admirable but in reality, humanly impossible! So, speaking strictly from a human standpoint, as well as scientifically, all we have said up to this point sounds like the teachings of one gone mad. However, in question is not man's ability, wisdom or power, but God's!

A perfect illustration of this is Jesus' teaching in Matthew 19:24-26. In that parable, a rich man had come to Jesus enquiring how he might gain eternal life. Jesus responded, "If thou wilt be perfect, go and sell that thou hast, and give to the poor, and thou shalt have treasure in heaven: and come and follow me" (Matthew 19:21).

Upon hearing Jesus' answer, the rich man left in sorrow because he could not bring himself to relinquish his wealth and possessions; even for eternal life. After that conversation, Jesus uttered these words, "It is easier for a camel to go through the eye of a needle, than for a rich man to enter into the kingdom of God" (Matthew 19:24).

Upon hearing this statement about the camel, the Disciples were astonished and asked, "Who then can be saved"? Their amazement sprang from the statement, "It is easier for a camel to go through the eye of a needle". According to Albert Barnes, the statement made in Matthew 19:24, was common among Jews to, "denote that a thing was impossible or exceedingly difficult". (Albert Barnes, *Barnes' Notes,* Matthew 19:16-30)

To such perceived impossibilities, Jesus responded, "With men this is impossible; but with God all things are possible" (Matthew 19:26).

This truth is just as applicable to the resurrection of the dead as it is to the Jewish proverb; nothing is impossible with God! God will *conform* all Christians to the image of His Son Jesus Christ; regardless of whether they are dead or alive (cf. I Thessalonians 4:14-18)!

The fifteenth chapter of First Corinthians is perhaps the clearest explanation of how God will accomplish this wondrous act. In the latter portion of the chapter, Paul gives a series of similes starting from verse thirty-seven and extending to verse forty-one.

In verses thirty-seven and thirty-eight, he start this discussion with the process involved in planting or sowing a seed of grain. The seed is buried in one form, but the end result; whether it is corn, barley, or wheat, is different from the sown seed, both in appearance and nature.

In verse thirty-nine, he draws another distinction between the flesh of humans, animals and birds. Though they are clothed in flesh, it is different for each category; there is one type of flesh for humanity, one type for animals, and one type for birds.

In verse forty, he goes one step further by comparing the bodies of celestial beings to that of terrestrial. In other words, the bodies of angels are not the same, either in composition, character or appearance as the bodies of terrestrial beings living on earth.

Finally, in verse forty-one, he draws a distinction between the glory of the sun to that of the moon and other smaller stars. These similes are designed to emphasize the sole fact that the body that is buried, cremated or lost at sea is in one form, but at the resurrection, they will be the same body in physical appearance only.

Paul highlights their differences in verses forty-two to forty-four by explaining the nature of the glorified or resurrected body as first being incorruptible. This new body will no longer be plagued by the curse of sin; it will be immortal and perfect in every sense of the word.

Not only will it be incorruptible, it will be honorable. The body buried in the earth was one of dishonor because it was conceived in sin. As such, it was plagued with disfigurement; scarring, blemishes and all manner of sicknesses, disease and pain. At the resurrection, this same body will be raised a *glorious* body! Free of all blemishes and fashioned like the glorious body of Christ.

Additionally, the *glorified* body is no longer subject to human weakness. Unlike animals, people do not have built into them natural defenses such as shells and other defense mechanisms to protect them from physical harm. People's bodies fall prey to all sorts of diseases and maladies.

The *glorified* body is not so! It is raised in power by the power of God. No longer needing food nor limited by space and distance. It will be able to yield the highest level of service to the Father and Son without becoming exhausted. But the greatest blessing of all, is the absence of death!

Finally, the *glorified* body is spiritual and not natural. In other words, the body we're born with is animal; that is, "being generated as animals are, and supported with food as they be, and die at last as they do". (John Gill, *John Gill's Exposition,* I Corinthians 15:45) Paul's point is that the nature of the resurrected and *glorified* body of the Christian will be uniquely different from the bodies we now have!

As such, our weak and frail bodies are *conformed* to the image of our Lord Jesus Christ. God transforms and glorifies it to the same likeness as was his son Jesus Christ at his resurrection! With his *glorified* body, Jesus appeared alongside his disciples on a road one moment and vanish from their sight the next (Luke 24:15-31); or walked through a closed and locked door (John 20:26). This is the character of the *glorified* body!

A NEED FOR CLARITY

Before proceeding, a particular aspect of this teaching involving the Christian being *conformed* to the image of Christ, or being *glorified,* must be clarified. The failure on the part of church leaders to do so have left individual Christians easy prey for false teachers who teach that we become 'little gods' when saved.

On the surface, Scripture seems to at least imply that reality. However, there is nothing further from the truth than such an interpretation. To classify such preachers and teachers, who teach such a damnable doctrine, as heretics would not be going too far. It is good for them that they live in a time of theological tolerance, because there was a time when such teachings were done at the risk of one's life! Fortunately for these false teachers, such severe punishment is no longer an issue in modern society.

Having said that, how then are we to understand this mysterious teaching surrounding our being *conformed* to the image of Jesus Christ?

First, it is a mystery almost as deep as that involving the Trinity itself, and one God has not chosen to disclose fully. While it's true, we read and can fairly grasp the concept of Jesus Christ being both God and man; our attempts eventually takes us to a place where finite intellect and knowledge ends. The reality is, our brain does not have the capacity to even come close to understanding this truth about our Lord; we simply accept it by faith.

Second, and perhaps more relevant to our present discussion is the fact that Jesus Christ is the second man or second Adam (I Corinthians 15:47). All of humanity, regardless of who they are, derived their nature from Adam! This fact is acceptable by all Christians and is the reason all of us are born sinners and in need of a savior. Dr. Martyn Lloyd-Jones helps us here by emphasizing that, "What happened in salvation is that we derive a new nature from this 'second man', this 'last Adam'". (Lloyd-Jones, *Romans: An Exposition of Chapter 8:17-39, 226*)

Dr. Lloyd-Jones's statement is clear! As long as we are in Adam's likeness, the possibility of being united to God is impossible! Therefore, if reconciliation is to take place, God must either change our nature or give us a new one. This is what happens at salvation, not that we get a new nature, but instead, we become part of another's—Jesus Christ! Though this issue of being part of our Lord's nature was discussed earlier, a look back on it is necessary to further help our understanding regarding how we are *conformed* to his image.

When we look at Scripture, the one phrase or statement that sums up the sole reason why Jesus came into the world is the angel Gabriel's words in Matthew's Gospel, ". . . he shall save his people from their sins", (Matthew 1:21b). Every act, from his birth to his resurrection, to his Second Coming, is the consummation of this one end, to "save his people from their sin". Therefore, when we think of the redemptive work of Jesus Christ, we must never limit our attention to any single act, but instead, see them all as one indivisible whole!

This is especially true when it comes to his humanity. It was not just that he is truly human, or that he lived a sinless life and died a horrible and agonizing death; all these facts are true, but we mustn't stop at them! We must connect the facets of his redemptive work to God's perfect plan to, "save his people from their sin". Such a focus naturally helps us understand and recognize the need for the new life given to us from Jesus Christ through the Holy Spirit (cf. John 3:3-6)!

This is Paul's teaching in the fifteenth chapter of I Corinthians in his statement, "As is the earthy, such are they also that are earthy: and as is the heavenly, such are they also that are heavenly" (v. 48). This verse brings out the universal truth set in place by God at creation (Genesis 1:11); like begets like. Adam could only generate sinners because that's what he became; it was his nature!

Likewise, and here is the crucial distinction, though Jesus Christ was born human, his conception was not through the seed of man, but the power of the Holy Spirit! The angel Gabriel declared to Mary, "The Holy Ghost shall come upon thee, and the power of the Highest shall overshadow thee: therefore also that holy thing which shall be born of thee shall be called the Son of God" (Luke 1:35). Since Jesus was coming to save human beings, he had to be born in our image and nature. This is the meaning behind the Hebrew writer's account, ". . . it is not possible that the blood of bulls and of goats should take away sins" (Hebrews 10:4). Since a man cast all humanity into sin, so must the redeemer be a man!

But what does all this have to do with the current discussion? Paul gives us the answer in First Corinthians Chapter fifteen and verse forty-five, "And so it is written, the first man Adam was made a living soul; the last Adam was made a quickening spirit". The first part of this verse is quoted from Genesis chapter two, verse seven with reference to Adam. The fact that Paul does not quote the Genesis passage verbatim does no harm to the integrity or inerrancy of God's Word; as the additions of 'first' and 'Adam' is done only to draw a distinction between Jesus and Adam.

This verse highlight the fact, Adam was made a living soul! By soul, Paul means that when God breathe into Adam's nostril, he became alive, animated, or better stated; the being made from clay became a breathing, animated, living creature! The whole point of the verse is to highlight and restate the single truth; all humanity bears the image of this breathing and animated being (I Corinthians 15:48).

The other relevant teaching taught in this verse centers around Jesus Christ as the second Adam'. Paul identifies both men as Adam to highlight the fact that both men generated a race of people. From Adam came the human race, conceived from his seed, ". . . in his own likeness, after his image" (Genesis 5:3).

God made Adam in His image, but Adam's sin corrupted that image. Since all of humanity was seminally present in him, all his descendants and their descendants would also be generated in his corrupt and sinful image and likeness. This is David's basis for declaring, "I was shapen in iniquity; and in sin did my mother conceive me", (Psalms 51:5).

Just as the human race has their origin in the first Adam, all Christians have theirs in the second Adam; Jesus Christ! The distinctive difference being, the second Adam, is a quickening Spirit. In other words, Adam needed the breath of God to have life. But this is not the case with our Lord, because he is life Himself and therefore, has the power to bestow life to others through his spirit! This is the meaning behind the term, 'quickening spirit'.

Jesus often declared this truth about himself in the Gospel of John (cf. John 1:4; 5:26; I Corinthians 15:21). Dr. Martyn Lloyd-Jones summarizes this truth in his word, "A race started in Adam, another race started in Christ". He goes on to say, "And the image to which you and I are to be made conformable is the image of the 'last Adam', that is to say, this perfect full humanity of the Lord Jesus Christ which is joined to his eternal sonship and Godhead". (Lloyd-Jones, *Romans: An Exposition of Chapter 8:17-39*, 227)

HOW ARE THE DEAD RESURRECTED

This brings us to the first question posed in I Corinthians 15:35, "How are the dead raised up"? This is also among the greatest mysteries in the Bible, and like others, God does not provide much detail. What He does tell us through the Apostle Paul is that, "We shall not all sleep, but we shall all be changed" (I Corinthians 15:51).

The meaning behind this verse is that not all Christians will sleep or die before the resurrection; or the rapture occurs. However, we shall all, be changed, or *glorified*. This is a declarative statement set forth to declare the certainty that all Christians will be *glorified*, regardless of whether they're alive or dead (I Thessalonians 4:14-18).

Another truth seen in this statement is the fact that the resurrection is not a necessary requirement of being *glorified*. In Paul's letter to the Christians at Thessalonica, he elaborates on this fact by providing the priority of those raptured on the last day. Paul's teaching in I Corinthians 15:52 supports the fact that the rapture, resurrection and *glorification* all takes place simultaneously.

However, in I Corinthians 15:51 Paul omits the question regarding those who are still alive when the resurrection occurs. That fact apparently troubled the Christians in the first century city of Thessalonica. Their concern along with false teachings moved Paul to write the fourth chapter of First Thessalonians.

In that letter, Paul spoke directly to this issue in order to assure the Christians living there that their love ones, who had already died, would experience the rapture with them. To help them understand how this was possible, and to dispel their fears, Paul comforted them with these words, "That we which are alive and remain unto the coming of the Lord shall not prevent them which are asleep", (I Thessalonians 4:15). The word used for 'prevent' in this verse does not mean 'stop', but 'go before'. He continues in verses sixteen and seventeen with the order of precedence, ". . . the dead in Christ shall rise first: Then we which are alive and remain shall be caught up together with them in the clouds, to meet the Lord in the air".

Do you see the order? Those who have died in Christ, or who accepted Christ as Savior, will rise first and be caught up, or raptured to be with the Lord; followed by those Christians who are alive at that time. Though we speak from the standpoint of precedence, the reality is that the whole process takes place, "In a moment, in the twinkling of an eye" (I Corinthians 15:52). Regarding this expression, Barnes writes, "This is an expression also denoting the least conceivable duration of time". (Albert Barnes, *Albert Barnes' Notes,* I Corinthians 15:42) So even though there is precedence, it will be indistinguishable.

But notice also, this takes place at the last Trumpet (I Thessalonians 4:16), which undoubtedly has reference to the Seven Trumpets spoken of in the book of Revelation. The controversy surrounding this event is not the subject of this book, its mentioning here is made only to further our understanding of *glorification.* For further information regarding the events of the rapture, the reader is encouraged to read the author's book entitled, *Lord, When.*

What a magnificent day this will be, when Jesus Christ returns for us! According to Jude, ten thousand angels will accompany Him (Jude 1:14). In the book of Revelation, the Apostle John tells us that Jesus Christ will come riding on a white horse with eyes, ". . . as a flame of fire, and on his head . . . many crowns" (Revelation 19:11, 12a).

Though these descriptions are but feeble attempts of the finite creature to describe the glory and splendor of our Lord's return, they still give us a reasonable idea of how brilliant and glorious this day will be for the Christian.

The resurrection, rapture, and glorification culminate our blessed hope. All the pain and suffering of this world will be gone! Trials and tribulations will be no more! Satan and temptation will be no more. Above all, we will not only see our blessed Savior, we will be *conformed* and united with him for eternity!

QUESTIONS TO PONDER

1. What is the significance of hope in understanding glorification?
2. Why does Paul speak of it as being the Christian's blessed hope in Titus 2:13?
3. Read I Corinthians 15:11-19 and answer the following:
   a. Why is Christ's resurrection important to the Christian faith?
   b. If Christ was not raised from the dead, what impact would it have on our faith and ultimately our own resurrection?
4. How does Paul describe the condition of the Christian who preach and teach the resurrection of Christ, if it did not happen?
5. How does Ephesians 5:30 help our understanding of being conformed to the image of Christ?

Epilog

The Function of the Church

Regarding the gospel, Dr. Martyn Lloyd-Jones said, "The Christian gospel is unique. It tells us: be what you are; realize what you are; and proceed to show that you are what you are". (Lloyd-Jones. D. M. *Romans, An Exposition of Chapter 12, Christian Conduct.* Edinburgh, Scotland: The Banner of Truth Trust, 2000, 113)

A careful consideration of Dr. Lloyd-Jones' statement reveals three facts about the Christian. First, Christians must be what they are. This prerequisite is significant because it determines the purpose of our existence. Of this, the Christians need not be confused since Jesus plainly declared us to be, ". . . the salt of the earth . . . and the light of the world" (Matthew 5:13, 14). That's what all Christians are salt and light to the world!

Unfortunately, far too many Christians fail to realize, understand, or accept this reality; but instead have resolved themselves to the task of bringing about social change and justice in the world through their own wisdom! They seem to forget or ignore the existence of countless secular organizations that not only have made this their struggle and focus, but whose fruit continuously manifests their ineffectiveness in resolving the myriad of problems plaguing humanity!

Our uniqueness as Christians is the exact thing needed by the world, especially in this hour where so much confusion exists regarding such issues as; marriage, abortion, crime, homosexuality, and the list could go on and on. If the world's mind frame is not altered and diverted to objective truths or principles that offer lasting solutions, its current hopelessness, despair and deterioration will continue its downward spiral.

This is why Christians must be what they are—salt and light! As salt and light, Christians act as a kind of preservative for society. (Lloyd-Jones, D. M. *Studies in The Sermon On The Mount.* Grand Rapids, Michigan:

Wm. B. Eerdman. 1971, 1976, 133) No other entity in any society, possesses this capability! All one need do is look at societies that prohibit and persecute Christians to see the reality of this statement! This point is missed when our Lord's statement in Matthew 5:13 is not examined carefully because what he actually said was, "ye, and ye alone, are the salt of the earth". (Lloyd-Jones, Sermon on the Mount, 112)

Do you see the importance of understanding the urgency behind our Lord's words? Does it not cry out—be what you are—that the world may be preserved! Consider for a moment Abraham's pleas to God to spare the cities of Sodom and Gomorrah (Genesis 18:20-19:25). Their preservation rested solely on Abraham's prayer and relationship to God. According to God's Word, if as little as ten righteous people could have been found, the cities would have been spared (cf. Genesis 18:23-33).

There was a time when Christians in America stood firm in their beliefs and unashamedly pointed out evil in society. As they lived godly lives and promoted the truths and principles of the gospel, they were acting as salt and light in the world. Because they understood 'what they were', functioning in society with relevance and purpose came easy. The evidence of their uniqueness manifested itself in their refusal to compromise in wrongdoings and intolerance of evil in any form clearly set them apart from those who were not Christians.

Christians are in the world; not to try and change it through our own insight, wisdom, or intellect. Instead, as salt and light, change is brought about as (through the Holy Spirit's indwelling power), Christians live out the gospel message among those around them. Such behavior will and impact families, neighborhoods and ultimately society as a whole.

No other passage of Scripture brings out this truth more clearly than God's Words to Solomon recorded in 2 Chronicles 7:14, "If my people, which are called by my name, shall humble themselves, and pray, and seek my face, and turn from their wicked ways; then will I hear from heaven, and will forgive their sin, and will heal their land". Do we want our country healed of its corruption and evil; then, Christian, 'be what you are'!

But notice the second fact revealed in Dr. Lloyd-Jones statement, Christians must realize, 'who they are'. I do not think by this phrase, Dr. Lloyd-Jones meant that Christians do not realize they are Christians. Instead, I believe he had in mind the idea that Christians do not fully comprehend all that is involved in being a Christian. In other words, they have not fully grasped the fact that being a Christian means, being united to Jesus Christ. Before being regenerated, they were dead and totally separated from him and without hope! But now, they are united in him (Romans 6:4-6); not symbolically, but in actuality.

As a result, we do not only represent him, we are his mystical body walking throughout our communities; places of employment, shopping centers, and among our friends and acquaintances. In essence, our bodies (by implication) are not our own! Paul puts it this way, ". . . nevertheless I live; yet not I, but Christ liveth in me: and the life which I now live in the flesh I live by the faith of the Son of God, who loved me, and gave himself for me" (Galatians 2:20b).

Christ lives in and through Christians! Therefore, everything done by the Christian is done through the power and might of Jesus Christ. This is the basis for focusing on the specific doctrines presented in this book; to remind us who God is, who we were before, and how it is that we have become part of the wonderful organism the Bible defines as the "Body of Christ"!

In other words, the reality of 'what we are' is based on our identity of 'who we are' as declared by Jesus Christ! Put another way, functionality is in view when talking about the 'what' of Christians; while identity or essence is in view when talking about 'who' the Christian is. Greater acceptance of these facts leads to saltier and brighter Christians; something the world is sorely in need of!

The Christian's understanding and full acceptance of their function and identity in society should naturally lead to 'showing that they are what they are'. And here lies the problem, because while many Christians enjoy the blessings of being who and what they are; it is when troubles and trials come that they find it difficult to express this reality to those around them. This goes back to what was said before about understanding what it means to be a Christian. Listen to our Lord's own words regarding the relationship between the Christian and the world, "If the world hate you, ye know that it hated me before it hated you. If ye were of the world, the world would love his own: but because ye are not of the world, but I have chosen you out of the world, therefore, the world hateth you" (John 15:18, 19).

The Christian who expect to be loved by the world clearly has not fully understood who they are. Mankind, especially the religious leaders of Jesus' time, hated him with every fiber of their being. People's feelings and opinions about Jesus today has not progressed significantly beyond those of the Pharisees and Sadducees who lived in the first century. Therefore, the world will never willingly join themselves to us or the cause of Jesus Christ unless acted upon by the Holy Spirit. This is the natural relationship between Christians and those who are not saved; mainly because each group's functionality is based on 'who they are'. Therefore, if there is to be any reconciliation between the two parties, the Christian must always be who they are.

Like the pain encountered when salt is applied to a wound, the world hates the Christian when their wickedness is pointed out and condemned. The same principle applies when light is shed on unbiblical truths such as; the senseless and brutal killings in our communities, drug abuse, political corruption, same sex marriage, abortion and all other evil committed against humanity. We cannot compromise on such issues; but must speak boldly against them because, it is our function and when properly carried out, society is preserved and strengthened. If for no other reason, this is why the Church should encourage its members to become part of every strata of society. When this happens, godly principles and influences can be brought to the discussion when laws and ordinance are being formulated and passed.

In making my previous statement, I must say up front, I do not believe, nor support the idea that the role of the local church is to insert itself into political and social issues directly. Instead, I believe the local church's primary function is to preach and teach the gospel of Jesus Christ to the unsaved people that come into her mist, so that the Holy Spirit can save those elected by God. Once saved, the local church's mission is to teach and train its people in biblical doctrine, which the Holy Spirit uses to transform their thinking to the point where they progressively come to an understanding of what and who they are. As they return to their respective roles in society, the biblical principles learned will manifest themselves in their daily actions as they yield themselves to the Holy Spirit's power. In other words, if the environment where the Christian works, live or socializes remains unaffected by their presence, there exists a strong possibility that, that Christian does not realize, or understand what and who they are.

We are Christians; that's who we are! But is this the testimony of friends, associates, and relatives; or do they see you as one of them? This is the essence of being salt and light. Jesus declared, ". . . if the salt have lost his savour, wherewith shall it be salted? It is thenceforth good for nothing, but to be cast out, and to be trodden under foot of men" (Matthew 5:13b). Do you see the seriousness of the Christian not realizing what and who they are? As stated earlier, the purpose of salt is to add flavor or to preserve. Light is given to provide light where darkness exists. Jesus' point then is clear, if neither is capable of performing its primary function, it is useless!

Therefore, the Christian must always be mindful of this one fact; whatever culture or environment they find themselves, remember that as salt, we act as preservatives and therefore must never lose our 'savour'. Once our savour is lost, our effectiveness upon our world is lost.

Even more so, when we fail to expose evil in any form, regardless how large or small it may appear; we cease being light to the world. Anyone who is honest with themselves will never deny the fact that the world today is filled with all manner of evil. One word used to describe evil, not just in the Bible, but even among those unsaved, is the word dark'. How often have we heard the expression, "he or she is from the dark side". Implied in such a statement is something evil or immoral. Christians understand evil in a way, unlike the world, because they have the truth and source of it as revealed to them through the word of God. Failure to shine our light allows evil to continue its reign and destruction of humankind.

This in itself would be tragic, but even more devastating would be the fact that the world would be deprived of hearing, learning and seeing the wondrous love that God has shown in sending his only begotten Son Jesus Christ to save them from their sin! It is my prayer and hope that this book will stimulate the Christian reader to the truth of knowing what you are so you can realize who you are; and begin to show the world that you are what you are. (Lloyd-Jones, Sermon on the Mount, 113) If this is done, maybe we can actually become the 'conscience of [our] society'.

BIBLIOGRAPHY

2 Timothy 3:13-17—Bible Study: Bible Study Guide. n.d. http://www.
biblestudyguide.org/comment/calvin/comm_vol43/htm/iv.iv.iii.htm
(accessed September 18, 2011).

Barackman, Floyd H. *Practical Christian Theology. Examining the Great
Doctrines of the Faith.* Third Edition. Grand Rapids, Michigan: Kregel
Publication, 1998.

Beyer, Bill T. Arnold & Bryan E. *Encountering the Old Testament, A
Christian Survey.* Second. Grand Rapids, Michigan: Baker Academic,
1999, 2008.

Calibria, John. *Syosset Central School District: Global History 9E.* January
15, 2000. http://homework.syossetistops.org/userimages/jcalabria/
Maps/Ancient_Near_East.jpg (accessed February 14, 2012).

Cobb, John J. *Lord, When? A Biblical Perspective on The Second Coming.*
Bloomington, Indiana: iUniverse, 2004.

Crystal, Ellie. *Crystalinks: Kings of Israel.* August 25, 1980. http://www.
crystalinks.com/kingsofisrael.html (accessed February 19, 2012).

Evans, Dr. Anthony T. *Spiritual Warfare.* Cassette Tape. Renaissance
Productions Inc. Wenonah, New Jersey, 1991.

Farlex. *The Free Dictionary by Farlex.* 2003. http://www.thefreedictionary.
com (accessed January 30, 2011).

Harcourt, Houghton Mifflin. "Houghton Mifflin History—Social
Science." *Houghton Mifflin World History—Ancient Civilization.* n.d.
http://www.utexas.edu/courses/classicalarch/images2/mapane.jpg
(accessed October 13, 2011).

Harrison, Rev. James M. *FOREKNOWLEDGE: There's More Than Meets
Gods Eye.* n.d. http://www.redmillsbaptist.org/foreknowledge.htm
(accessed September 25, 2009).

Herbert Lockyer, DD. *All the Divine Names and Titlles in the Bible.* Grand
Rapids, Michigan: Zondervan Publishing House, 1975.

MacArthur, John F Jr. *The Vanishing Conscience, Drawing The Line In A No-Fauly, Guilt-Free World*. Dallas, London, Vancouver, Melbourne: Word Publishing, 1994.

Josephus, Flavius. *The Complete Works of Josephus*. Translated by Wm. Whiston. Grand Rapids, Michigan: Kregal Publications, 1981.

Lloyd-Jones, D. Martyn. *Romans, An Exposition of Chapter 5: Assurance*. Grand Rapids, Michigan: Zondervan Publishing House, 1971.

—. *Romans, An Exposition of Chapter 8:17-39, The final perseverence of The Saints*. Edingburg, Scotland: The Banner of Truth Trust, 1998.

—. *Romans: An Exposition of Chapter 9, God's Sovereign Purpose*. Edinburgh, Scotland: The Banner of Truth Trust, 1991.

—. *Romans: An Exposition of Chapters 3:20-4:25, Atonement and Justification*. Grand Rapids, Michigan: Zondervan Publishing House, 1970.

—. *Studies in the Sermon on the Mount*. Second. 1 vols. Grand Rapids, Michigan: Wm. Eerdmans Publishing Company, 1971, 1976.

Meyer, Rick. "Jamieson, Faussett and brown Commentary." *e-sword*. Rick Meyer. (2000-2009). http://www.e-sword.net (accessed 2010-2011).

—. "John Gill's Complete Exposition of The Bible." *e-sword*. 2000-2009. http://www.e-sword.net (accessed October 15, 2010).

Meyers, Rick. "International Standard Bible Enclyclopedia." *e-sword*. 2000-2009. http://www.e-sword.net (accessed 2010-2011).

—. "International Standard Bible Enclyclopedia." *e-sword*. 2000-2009. http://www.e-sword.net (accessed October 31, 2010).

—. *Kiel & Delitzsch Commentary on the Old Testament*. (2000-2009). http://www.e-sword.net (accessed November 11, 2010).

Myers, Rick. "Albert Barnes' Notes on The Bible." *e-Sword*. Rick Myers. 2000-2009. http://www.e-sword.net (accessed 2010-2011).

Oswalt, John S. *The New International Commentary on the Old Testament (NICOT), The Book of Isaiah Chapters 1-39*. Grand Rapids, Michigan: William B. Eerdmans Publishing Company, 1986.

Pentecost, Dwight W. *Things That Become Sound Doctrine*. Grand Rapids, Michigan: Kregel Publications, 1965.

Pink, Arthur W. *The Attributes of God*. Grand Rapids: Baker Books, 1975.

Renick, Timothy M. *Aquinas, For Armchair Theologians*. 1st. Louisville, London: Westminster John Knox Press, 2002.

Sproul, R. C. *Chosen By God.* Wheaton, Illinois: Tyndale House Publishers, inc., 1986.

—. *Faith Alone, The Evangelical Doctrine of Justification.* Grand Rapids: Baker Books, 1995.

—. *The Mystery of the Holy Spirit, Discover the Work of The Living Spirit of the Living God.* Wheaton, Illinois: Tyndale House Publishers, Inc., 1990.

Venning, Ralph. *The Sinfulness of Sin.* Edingburgh, Scotland: The Banner of Truth Trust, 1997.

INDEX